W9-BPS-291

Reform
of
Undergraduate
Education

Arthur Levine

John Weingart

REFORM OF UNDER-GRADUATE EDUCATION

Jossey-Bass Publishers
San Francisco • Washington • London • 1973

REFORM OF UNDERGRADUATE EDUCATION
by Arthur Levine and John Weingart

JACKET DESIGN BY WILLI BAUM

FIRST EDITION

Code 7328

The
Jossey-Bass Series
in Higher Education

Preface

In 1969–1970, while we were seniors at Brandeis University, we both held student-government offices and therefore served on most student, faculty, administration, trustee, and alumni education committees. Though we look back on that period warmly, most of the time we were frustrated. Each week at the Brandeis Educational Policy Committee someone would insist that the future of the university rested on our dropping a given requirement or adding a proposed program. And each week we traded anecdotes and guesses about the effects of the proposals. The most compelling arguments were based on the experience of a relative or a friend or a friend of a relative at another school where the proposal or something like it had been adopted. Through the magic of parliamentary procedure, we were able to resolve the same issue at several consecutive meetings with any number of different conclusions. Everybody had an equal chance to win, and everybody did one week or another. But when a proposal went to the faculty for final approval, we all stood behind it. The faculty then repeated the same discussions that we had had and voted in their own way, basing their votes on their own feelings and their own anecdotes. And the resolutions that came out of the faculty meetings became educational policy.

The situation at Brandeis is not unique. Anybody who has sat on a committee has had similar experiences. Committees do not typically seek out information to solve problems; they try to form a consensus. During our last few months at Brandeis we became aware that most colleges have the same curriculum and make educational policy in the same way that Brandeis does. We thought that if colleges—administrators, faculties, and students—had concrete information about how the programs they are considering have functioned at other schools, educational decision making could have a base other than the last and most eloquent voice.

We therefore decided to study undergraduate programs at twenty-six colleges, including Brandeis. The specific programs, the specific colleges, and other preliminary details of our study are discussed in Chapter One.

Our emphasis was on the need for reform and on current attempts at reform—in seven major areas. We devote a chapter to each of these areas, describing the alternatives available and the strengths and weaknesses of each alternative. Our conclusion is that attempts at reform, however stimulating and numerous and creative and hopeful, are at loggerheads almost everywhere with traditions—traditional student passivity and traditional university reward systems that extol specialization and concentration.

Because this book is structured as it is, it makes a convenient "plumber's manual" for colleges considering curriculum changes. That is, from the discussions in each chapter a college can select the curriculum structure that best suits its needs. However, as we note in Chapter One and also in Chapter Nine, piecemeal reform is less effective than a wholesale reform based on a coherent philosophy.

Chapters Two through Eight concentrate on the seven areas that are currently undergoing reforms. Chapter Two considers the current status of academic advising. Here we are forced to conclude that advising is still a vast wasteland, primarily because advisors are given no incentives for this task and know little about a university outside their specialties.

Chapter Three discusses programs in general education—

that is, the various attempts made to ensure breadth in the undergraduate experience. Here we focus on core courses, such as the Contemporary Civilization course at Columbia; distribution requirements; freshman seminars—as held at Sarah Lawrence, Stanford, Trinity College, Haverford College, Brown University, and Harvard; and various special programs such as Directed Studies at Yale, the Experimental College Program at Berkeley, and the great books approach at St. John's. Chapter Four, on comprehensive examinations and senior-year activities, continues this emphasis on breadth, discussing the attempts by sample colleges to get students to review, gain perspective, stop short, and see where they have been and where they are going at various stages of their college careers. In general, we found that almost all attempts at breadth are hindered by the traditional university emphasis on specialization and concentration.

Chapter Five, on concentration (or the selection of a major), assesses the various ways (for instance, through double majors, joint majors, interdepartmental majors, and student-created majors) that colleges and universities have been attempting to loosen concentration requirements and make them meaningful to students. Such attempts, so far, have been only marginally successful—often because only a few students have used the opportunities available to them.

Chapter Six, "Alternatives to Departments," and Chapter Seven, "Student-Centered Curriculum," discuss further attempts at loosening strict departmental structures and making courses and programs individually meaningful to students. The alternatives to departments considered are alternative faculty structures (as at Prescott, the University of California at Santa Cruz, and the University of Wisconsin at Green Bay) and extradepartmental programs, such as the Flexible Curriculum program at Brandeis and similar more extensive extradepartmental programs at Stanford, Tufts, and Yale. The student-centered curricula discussed are various student-teaching opportunities and independent-study programs.

Chapter Eight notes the attempts being made to make grading systems more personalized and meaningful and less pressure-laden and traditional, through written evaluations, oral evaluations, and various pass-fail systems. The obstacle to such systems remains the emphasis of graduate and professional schools on so-called objective traditional letter or numerical grades.

Our final chapter seeks to put all our specific findings in perspective by analyzing the general character of students, faculty, and administrators as we observed it during our many interviews, discussions, and tours of selected campuses.

We would like to thank Robert S. Benjamin, Robert Boas, the David J. Greene Foundation, Steven Resnick, Edward Rose, and the Brandeis University Student Council for their financial assistance. In addition, we are grateful to Dale Morse for her help in preparing and evaluating our data; to Norman Abrams, Jacob Cohen, Michael Eig, Hans Flexner, Barbara Goldman, Emily Hotaling-Eig, John Matthews, Richard V. McCann, Deborah Spitalnik, Jonathan R. Warren, and Richard Weckstein for their advice in revising our manuscript; to Steve Cupp, Phyllis Erico, Bernard Levinson, David Squire, and Jerry Weinstein for their helping hands; to Dorothy Conway and JB Hefferlin of Jossey-Bass; to Kenneth D. Benne, whose insights showed us what education could be. And we dedicate this book to William Goldsmith, our friend and teacher.

Buffalo, New York   ARTHUR LEVINE
Princeton, New Jersey   JOHN WEINGART
September 1973

Contents

xiii

Contents

Reform
of
Undergraduate
Education

Current Undergraduate Programs

$$T$$he four-year college curriculum has become standardized since the end of World War II. Even the so-called experimental colleges are variations on the same theme. This curriculum consists of both a breadth and a depth component. The breadth is provided by liberal or general education, and the depth is provided by concentration. At the same time, and within this general framework, many attempts at reform have been and continue to be made; and much of this reform in higher education is aimed at providing students with a more personalized education.

Since we realized at the outset that a study of twenty-six institutions could not do justice to all curricular offerings in undergraduate colleges, we imposed some necessary limitations. We decided to study only three- and four-year liberal arts colleges, and we excluded schools with student-faculty ratios smaller than five to one. We then tried to make as representative a selection as possible,

1

Table 1. Sample Schools and Programs in Undergraduate Education

	Interviewees[a]			
	Students	Faculty	Admin.	Data-Collection Techniques
ANTIOCH COLLEGE Yellow Springs, Ohio (1850 stu., 100 fac.; Feb 71)[b]	100	25	3	Work-study program. Student body is divided into two groups: one group on campus, the other involved in field experience.
BARD COLLEGE Annandale-on-Hudson, N.Y. (625 stu., 60 fac.; March 71)	60	19	2	
BOWDOIN COLLEGE Brunswick, Maine (946 stu., 120 fac.; Dec 70)	43	7	3	Senior seminars; interviewees are a sample of senior-seminar students (class size in fall 1970: 230) and faculty (professors leading seminars in fall 1970: 19).
BRANDEIS UNIVERSITY Waltham, Mass. (2300 u., 725 g., 300 fac.; May 70)[c]	6	6	3	Flexible Curriculum Committee; interviewees are all the student and faculty members and three involved administrators of this committee.
BROWN UNIVERSITY Providence, R. I. (3391 u., 1493 g., 750 fac.; Dec 70, March 71)	225	60	4	Curriculum revision of 1969: In Dec. 1970 had 20 interviews with faculty, students, administration involved. Modes of Thought (MOT) courses: March 1971 interviews were with sample students and administration in MOT and with 40 faculty teaching MOT and 20 faculty not.
CALIF. INSTITUTE OF TECHNOLOGY Pasadena, Calif. (722 u., 762 g., 660 fac.; Jan 71)	76	17	3	Change in grading system for freshman courses. Faculty interviewed had taught freshman courses before and after the grading change.

Institution				Description
COLUMBIA UNIVERSITY New York, N.Y. (4620 u., 9000 g., 1500 fac.; Dec 70, March 71)	0	19	3	Contemporary Civilization courses. Faculty interviewed were 14 of the 27 teaching the courses in 1970–71 and 5 faculty responsible for staffing the courses. Student opinions secured through course-evaluation findings.
ECKERD COLLEGE St. Petersburg, Fla. (1080 stu., 80 fac.; April 71)	108	23	0	Core program in general education. Faculty interviewed include 3 in administrative positions.
HARVARD UNIVERSITY Cambridge, Mass. (5679 stu., 1575 fac.; Nov 70)	100	14	0	Freshman-seminar program (with approximately 700 students and 40–50 faculty each year). Interviewees were program participants for 1969–70.
HAVERFORD COLLEGE Haverford, Pa. (600 stu., 85 fac.; April 71)	60	20	2	Freshman-seminar program; 75% of faculty interviewed had participated in this program. Students were mainly freshmen and sophomores.
MASS. INSTITUTE OF TECHNOLOGY Cambridge, Mass. (3900 u., 3800 g., 700 fac.; Dec 70)	—	—	—	Unified Science Study Program (USSP). Interviewees are administration staff of this program. Students not available for interview; data derived largely from Schwartz and Morgan (see Bibliography, under MIT).
JUSTIN MORRILL COLLEGE East Lansing, Mich. (850 stu., 32 fac.; Nov 70)	50	8	1	Residential college of Michigan State University. Student interviewees were freshmen and sophomores (approximately 10% of those at the college). Four of the faculty interviews were arranged by the administrator.
NEW COLLEGE Sarasota, Fla. (500 stu., 52 fac.; April 71)	50	20	0	New College is designed to offer a three-year baccalaureate; however, many students take four years.
PRESCOTT COLLEGE Prescott, Ariz. (300 stu., 44 fac.; Jan 71)	57	20	1	Interdisciplinary teaching and research centers.

Table 1. SAMPLE SCHOOLS AND PROGRAMS IN UNDERGRADUATE EDUCATION (Cont.)

	Interviewees[a]			Data-Collection Techniques
	Students	Faculty	Admin.	
REED COLLEGE Portland, Ore. (1100 stu., 100 fac.; Jan 71)	75	25	3	Core course: Introduction to Modern Humanities.
ST. JOHN'S COLLEGE Annapolis, Md. (350 stu., 48 fac.; April 71)	47	16	3	Great books program.
SARAH LAWRENCE COLLEGE Bronxville, N.Y. (553 stu., 110 fac.; March 71)	50	24	0	
STANFORD UNIVERSITY Stanford, Calif. (6078 u., 5244 g., 967 fac.; Jan 71)	76	26	0	Freshman-seminar program and various extra-departmental programs, such as Stanford Workshops on Political and Social Issues (SWOPSI).
TRINITY COLLEGE Hartford, Conn. (1400 stu., 110 fac.; March 71)	100	34	2	Freshman-seminar program. Of faculty interviewees, 29 were selected randomly from list of more than 50 program participants; the remaining 5 were randomly selected to round out divisional representations. Of student interviewees, about 2/3 were freshmen-sophomores; 1/3 juniors-seniors.
TUFTS UNIVERSITY Medford, Mass. (2322 u., 2747 g., 300 fac.; May 71)	—	—	—	Tufts Experimental College. Information derived largely from extensive interviews with coordinator of the college and a student member of the governing board. Other information contained in literature (see Bibliography, under Tufts).

Institution				Notes
UNIVERSITY OF CALIF., BERKELEY Experimental College Program (150 stu., 12 fac.; Jan–Feb 71)	25	6	0	Experimental College Program, temporarily terminated 1969. Interviewees are drawn from both of the two-year cycles of the program. Some interviews obtained through mailed questionnaires.
UNIVERSITY OF CALIFORNIA, SANTA CRUZ Santa Cruz, Calif. (3000 u., 225 g., 250 fac.; Jan 71)	135	45	8	Individual colleges (five operating 1971; only three—Cowell, Crown, Stevenson—examined in study). Interviewees include 15 faculty and 45 students from each college. Total population: 600 students, 40–50 faculty per college.
UNIVERSITY OF MICHIGAN RESIDENTIAL COLL. Ann Arbor, Mich. (900 stu., 85 fac.; Nov 70)	—	—	—	Residential College data obtained primarily from reports by Francis and Moore (see Bibliography, under University of Michigan).
UNIVERSITY OF WISCONSIN, GREEN BAY Green Bay, Wisc. (4000 stu., 260 fac.; Feb 71)	—	—	—	New campus with entire curriculum focused on the environment. Programs here are too new for evaluation. We attempted to show only how program operates. Interviews were not random and were few in number.
WESLEYAN UNIVERSITY Middletown, Conn. (1450 stu., 300 fac.)	—	—	—	Grading system. Information obtained from report by McMahon, Haagen, and Adamany (see Bibliography, under Wesleyan).
YALE UNIVERSITY New Haven, Conn. (4000 u., 4365 g., 900 fac.; March 71)	0	35	0	Residential college seminars and Directed Studies program. Faculty interviewees were about 25% of faculty participating in each of these programs in spring 1970. Student information derived mainly from *Yale Course Critique* (see Bibliography, under Yale).

a Interviewees randomly selected, unless otherwise indicated. Among students, few freshmen (and no graduate students) interviewed unless otherwise indicated. For literature used in addition to the interviews see bibliography items listed under the various institutions.

b Dates given are dates of campus visits and interviews.

c Abbreviations: u. = undergraduate students; g. = graduate students.

choosing schools that sponsored several programs of interest, were of manageable size for interviewing, and were geographically feasible to visit. Table 1 lists the schools that we finally selected, as well as special aspects of the data collection at each school.

The actual study had two components—the human and the numerical. The human component—what it is like to be part of a program—was obtained by interviews with students, faculty, and administrators. The numerical component was derived from statistics compiled for each program by a registrar or an office of institutional research. The statistical data desired for concentration or major, for instance, consisted of the number of people majoring in each department and in interdisciplinary programs, the number of students creating their own majors, the topics of these majors, and feedback from graduate and professional schools and employers. Thus, a picture of what happened was obtained through statistics, and the reasons why were obtained through interviews.

The technique employed in interviewing a college population was random selection of at least 10 percent of the students involved in a given program (much larger percentages for smaller programs), random selection of 20 percent to 25 percent of the faculty who had taught in the program for the past year or term (again, larger percentages for smaller programs), and discussions with the various administrators involved. The numbers 10 percent and 20 percent were chosen because they were the largest sample that we felt we could reasonably interview as a result of time and sanity limitations on the project; however, these numbers were sufficient to give an adequate picture of student and faculty opinion. We achieved randomness in student sampling by interviewing in many different places, including dormitories, hangouts, libraries, dining halls, snack bars, and book stores. The dean of student's office, school newspaper editors, and student-government leaders were useful in providing information about student living arrangements and social habits. In schools with large off-campus populations, we conducted more of our interviews in public places than in dormitories, in order not to lose an important segment of the student population.

We randomly selected faculty from a list of those who had participated in programs of interest (selecting, say, every fourth name or every tenth name on the list). The only restriction was that representation be given to each division of the school—usually social science, humanities, and natural science. This restriction resulted in special consideration at only one school, Stanford University. Larger percentages were interviewed in small programs, where 10 percent and 25 percent amounted to only a few individuals; in the Experimental College Program at Berkeley, for instance, we interviewed 54 percent of the faculty (six people) and 30 percent of the students (twenty-five people). In contrast, at large universities slightly smaller percentages were interviewed; at Brown University, for instance, only 8 percent of the students and 15 percent of the faculty were interviewed. In addition, at eight colleges some portion of the examination procedure was omitted because the desired information was available through institutional research of satisfactory design. The data in each case were inspected closely before the research was accepted. At three other colleges we had to replicate studies because the research design deviated from that desired.

Various methods of interviewing were attempted. Initially, written questionnaires were circulated (the procedure used at the Residential College of the University of Michigan); however, this procedure proved less than optimal. At Justin Morrill College, therefore, we used uniform open-ended questions and took notes. Open-ended questions proved more successful than questionnaires, but note-taking proved inefficient. At Harvard University, therefore, we conducted cassette tape-recorded interviews, and this procedure proved to be satisfactory. We then continued the use of open-ended questions and tape-recorded interviews for the duration of the research.

When we began our study, we made certain assumptions. First of all, we assumed, programs that permit students to plan their own education would be very successful in the creation of thoughtful, innovative student programs and independent student learning. In addition, team-taught and interdisciplinary programs would be considered more exciting and more enlightening by students in integrating the knowledge that is divided by the disciplines. Again, faculty would enjoy the change of pace arising from such programs. Written evaluations of student performances would prove to be a satisfactory means of providing the enriched feedback that students seek. And finally, no pattern of student and faculty behaviors would emerge; rather, each structure examined would have its unique strengths and weaknesses.

Our predictions were a disaster. Contrary to our expectations, we found that students do not participate in programs that permit them to plan their own education. Interdisciplinary and team-taught programs often fail because faculty do not want to teach them. When faculty do teach them, they are unable to integrate their disciplines or to work together. Written evaluations are also unsuccessful because faculty find them too burdensome, students are not interested in them, and graduate schools dislike them. Finally, student and faculty performance—whether in interdisciplinary and team-taught courses, student-centered curriculum, written-evaluation grading, or any other structure—proved to be much the same in each program examined.

Perhaps some of these findings are the result of the manner in which changes were made rather than the quality of the changes as such. That is, most of the programs examined at the twenty-six sample schools represented piecemeal change. The effect of even a number of the curricular changes at any one school was rarely more than the sum of its parts. Thus, Haverford College, which sponsored some of the most innovative and successful curricular structures found, can be described only as "having fairly standard academic offerings with the following distinctive features: . . ." Because the changes were piecemeal and not parts of a coherent whole program, we could easily isolate freshman seminars at Harvard, or freshman grading at the California Institute of Technology, and ignore the rest of the school's program. The only schools where such an approach was not possible were St. John's, which incorporates unique curricular mechanisms into a total academic program, and the Experimental College Program at Berkeley.

Since piecemeal reforms consistently ignore, and in fact are often destroyed by, the most basic problems afflicting higher education—problems such as the faculty reward system and the student's experiences prior to college, one must consider why such reforms are undertaken and what they are worth. They are initiated because they are relatively easy to adopt. An individual or group dissatisfied with the academic program often decides that a small change or addition will make a difference. Because such changes seldom threaten university life styles, they are sometimes approved. Reforms that confront the total curriculum are harder to enunciate and rarely possible to have adopted; so they are not proposed seriously.

Nevertheless, such reforms are often surprisingly successful, frequently because they represent a change. The often-raised argument that a proposed reform is "only change for change's sake" can be turned around to a proposal's advantage. Faculty members who teach the same course at the same school for five or ten years can become bored, and the boredom can quickly permeate an institution. Much like the Hawthorne effect—that is, the improvement in output of factory workers if they are given special attention regardless of its form (see Roethlisberger and Dickson, 1947)—minor changes at colleges can have a salutary effect by altering the annual routine. To demonstrate the applicability of the Hawthorne effect to the colleges, one has only to look at freshman-seminar programs. Faculty participants in such programs consistently said that the seminar was a radical new idea, permitting them endless opportunities for course experimentation. But when all the rhetoric is cut away, the freshman seminar is only a small class offered by a teacher. At any time instructors could have taught the same course with limited enrollment, but they didn't think of it because they are conditioned to assume that experimentation does not occur in traditional courses. Even if freshman seminars had been offered on an ad hoc basis, the students, who inherit faculty assumptions and attitudes, probably would not have regarded them as anything special. So, if official sanction produces more interesting courses with happier professors and students, universities have a responsibility to change for change's sake.

However, piecemeal reform presents two immediate dangers. First, constant change can exact a toll in security; for instance, students and faculty at Prescott College, where the curriculum was not yet stabilized, and at Eckerd College, where the core program changed frequently, complained of too much change, causing them anxiety. Students were unable to make short-range plans and faculty were unable to prepare course material adequately because their programs were in such flux. The second threat posed by piecemeal reform is that it will be accepted as a sufficient and satisfactory approach to college curriculum. Permitting students to create their own majors does little to solve the problem of overspecialization and professionalism of professors; and altering the advising or grading system does not adequately confront the fact that many students in college feel no purpose in being there. Piecemeal reform is clearly less desirable than a broad confrontation with the nature and purpose of college. But if minor changes, in addition to their specific merits, force people to break a few of the habits through which they sleepwalk each day and stimulate a reexamination of their role in the college, and perhaps of the college's role in the world, then piecemeal reform and change for its own sake are preferable to no change at all. But even the best piecemeal structures ultimately fail because of the fundamental lack of coherence and purpose characterizing such planning (see Chapter Nine). Colleges would be more successful in the long run if they geared their planning to a comprehensive overview of education, based upon the actualities of their school and the philosophy underlying it.

2

Advising

When thinking of advising programs, we remember especially an interview with one administrator who said, "There are six advisors for the 4800 freshmen here." "You mean, each advisor has 800 students?" "No," the administrator replied, "we like to think each student has six advisors."

Until recently universities have clearly distinguished between the affective and cognitive components of learning, emphasizing the cognitive almost entirely. This division is still present in most university counseling programs, manifest in a separation between academic and personal advising programs. Academic advising was studied at Antioch, Bard, Brown, Haverford, Justin Morrill, New College, Prescott, Reed, Santa Cruz, Sarah Lawrence, and Trinity.

Nine of the schools employ a two-part advising system designed to mirror the general education/concentration division. Sarah Lawrence and New College differ from this model in that their programs do not require concentration (see Chapter Five). At all the schools the freshman is assigned to a faculty advisor for the lower college years of general education. At a majority of these

schools, assignment is based upon preliminary major choice; however, New College uses student hobbies and interests as the basis for
advisor selection, and Haverford, Sarah Lawrence, and Trinity
assign the students to their Freshman Seminar instructor. After the
student declares a major, academic advising becomes the responsibility of the concentration unit. All units assign advisors to students,
and many permit students to change advisors as often as desired. At
Sarah Lawrence and New College, the assignment of the postfresh-
man advisor is based upon criteria important to the student.

Most of the faculty, students, and especially administrators
interviewed in our study described the advising as poor. Though a
large number of students, rarely a majority, had had positive experiences with their advisor, only very rarely did a student comment
that he and his advisor had developed a good relationship. The
assignment of advisors on the basis of a student's potential major
choice or indicated interest seems insufficient to foster such a relationship—particularly since many students oscillate between different majors. Not surprisingly, therefore, as many as three fifths of
the students at each of the schools chose not to see their advisor, and
a significant number of students indicated instead a preference for
obtaining advice from administrators, faculty, and student friends.

This problem is ameliorated slightly at Bard, New College,
and Prescott, which are so small that, according to faculty and students interviewed, everyone gets to know at least some students or
faculty well. Similarly, many credited the size for producing an informal environment, which encourages easier discussion. At New
College the informality exists to such a large extent that casual
advising replaces, in practice, the planned system. At Bard almost
all the faculty know the college and their colleagues well enough to
feel competent giving advice in most areas or telling students where
to get any information they need. Larger size, as might be expected,
produces opposite results, worsening an already poor system. Because
of increased size, at schools such as Brown, one of the larger and
more rigorously departmentalized of the schools, faculty tend to
know few of their colleagues—often only professors in their own or
closely allied departments.

No incentive is offered faculty members for advising at the
eleven schools. As a result, advising is looked upon as an obligation

that takes up time better spent on work that is rewarded. Consequently, the advising chore is given in heaping helpings to junior faculty. This means that the instructors with the least experience in a school are the ones who most often participate in advising. The problem is most severe when a first-year faculty member, knowing as little about the college as the student, is assigned to advising. A significant number of students attributed the failure of their advising relationship to this situation.

Only at Sarah Lawrence did the faculty interviewed appear to have a serious commitment to advising, considering it one of the main responsibilities of their job. Advising time there occupies about a day and a half per week. Students and faculty at Sarah Lawrence were more enthusiastic about their advising system than the participants at any other school. The faculty did complain, however, that they had too many students (often more than fifteen) to advise.

Another problem at the various schools is the lack of a clear notion of the advisor's role. Faculty and students interviewed often had very different notions. Some said that the advisor performs an administrative function; others said that he provides academic information; still others said that he is a tutor, or a personal counselor, or a friend. A problem is created, for example, when a student who wants a friend is paired with an advisor who wants to perform an administrative function. Perhaps the best method for assigning advisors would be based upon similarly defined advising functions by faculty and students.

Some students complained, "My advisor is never around." Many others insisted that they did not need an advisor because they felt competent to plan their own academic program; even if the advising system were improved, such students probably still would not participate. The remaining problems indicated by students and faculty resulted largely from personal interaction. Poor relationships caused by personality differences were common.

As could be expected, advising was viewed as far worse in the general education area than in concentration. However, after five of the sample schools had made renovations in general education advising, the major advising system, once felt to be superior, was perceived as a dismal failure—which indicates that major advising is not adequate, but only relatively better than general education advising.

In short, all undergraduate advising systems, with the exception of Sarah Lawrence's, are grossly inadequate. (The following sections discuss alternatives designed to improve advising.)

Compulsory Advising

Most schools impose advising upon students and faculty by requiring that student programs and administrative petitions be approved by an advisor. In addition, Santa Cruz and Reed force the students to consult their advisors to obtain written evaluations and grade reports. Compulsory advising evidently does promote greater student-faculty contact; to a lesser extent, the advisor does help to monitor student programs; and for very few students such advising has prevented severe mistakes. However, it simultaneously undermines the advising system. Advising, by virtue of its required administrative role, becomes routinized and transformed into an entirely administrative structure. Many students admitted that they contact their advisor to obtain his signature five minutes before semester programs are due. Others complained of going to their advisor with a problem only to have the advisor reach for a pen and ask "What has to be signed?" Abuses—students forging the signature of an advisor, advisors authorizing secretaries to sign program cards were occasionally noted as well. On the other hand, a relatively small number of students said that only because of the compulsory consultations had they met their advisor and subsequently developed a good relationship.

Student Advisors

Brown and Justin Morrill both supplement the faculty advising structure with student advisors. At Justin Morrill lower-division advising is performed primarily by upperclassmen chosen by a student-faculty board. Offices are set aside for student advising, which makes advisors readily available. Student advisors are salaried, receiving about $1.75 an hour for at least ten hours a week. At this rate a salaried program employing only ten advisors would cost at least seven thousand dollars a year.

willingness to participate in, freshman-seminar programs (see Chapter Three).

Freshman Inquiry

In 1971 Haverford introduced a group advising session, called Freshman Inquiry, occurring at the end of the freshman year. Freshmen are required to prepare a 1500-word essay for the Inquiry on "their current intellectual position and a justified plan for their future course of study." Each student then meets with a board consisting of a senior student and a faculty member from each academic division of the college, including the student's premajor advisor. The board is charged with suggesting changes in the student's plans, approving his plans, or requiring the student to repeat the Inquiry. Written copies of the board's assessment are filed with the student's advisor and the registrar, though not as part of the student's public record.

Three quarters of the participating faculty, freshmen, and seniors liked the Inquiry, and very few were critical. Two thirds of the faculty felt that the Inquiry is a helpful extension of advising. Other strengths cited by faculty include additional advising contact, the opportunity to learn by watching one's advisees react with other faculty, and the opportunity for students to meet new faculty and receive additional advice. The major drawback, according to faculty, is the amount of time required by the Inquiry itself. One fifth characterized the sessions as very tiring, and one student even felt that his Inquiry had failed because the panel was so tired.

Initiation of such a program at universities with student-faculty ratios larger than Haverford's may be impossible if it requires increasing the number of students each committee must see, since even Haverford's two-day Inquiry was described as exhausting. Lengthening the duration of the Inquiry would increase expenses by eating into course time, although such a sacrifice might perhaps be worthwhile.

A successful program is highly dependent upon a proper faculty attitude and a willingness to commit the necessary time to the Inquiry. Furthermore, an Inquiry program must be clearly defined to the understanding of all participants before it is adopted. A high level of anxiety was noted by many Haverford students and faculty, attributable to a lack of adequate information and the prevalence of rumors regarding the Inquiry session. Utilization of a trial period prior to the wholesale adoption of such a program is desirable. Haverford undertook a series of public trial inquiries in 1969–1970 and, on the basis of the inadequacies in the sessions, changed the nature of the Inquiry significantly.

Though receiving by far the most positive response of all advising mechanisms discussed, and incurring the least expense, the Inquiry has strict limitations. The most obvious problem is that the session is a "one-shot deal." After a student's hour before the board, the feedback from the group is over, although a few students indicated that they planned to maintain contact with board members other than their advisor.

Conclusion

Academic advising was shown to be uniformly unsuccessful at all the schools studied except Sarah Lawrence, where faculty are recruited and rewarded for their dedication to students. However, the Sarah Lawrence system requires an enormous faculty time commitment, which most colleges would consider prohibitive. Elsewhere, advising was unable to serve the minimal function of providing students with sufficient knowledge to use the resources of the college most advantageously. While administrators at each school almost always spoke of the need for improved advising, few schools were even aware of what they would expect from a good advising system. All the advising structures discussed did improve advising somewhat but failed to attack the basic problem; that is, faculty are rewarded largely for research and teaching in their specialty, so that their interests necessarily exclude advising. In addition, they are incompetent as nonmajor advisors, since they know nothing about the college outside their department. So, the many administrators who smiled and said "We're introducing a new advisory system next year" are going to be equally unhappy in the coming year, because tinkering with the mechanics of the system does not attack the basic problem with the faculty. A more promising approach is that being attempted at Manhattanville College in New York, in which advising is considered part of an instructor's course load.

Advising also suffers as universities increase the size of their student bodies and decrease the size of their faculties. The pressure of increased numbers has forced the simplification of advising to the point that the affective component has been eliminated, in favor of the more easily tended cognitive component. To create a more useful and effective relationship, advising must look at the whole student, initiate new methods of advisor assignment, and provide better opportunities for the growth of the advising relationship. In view of the failure of almost all advising structures to provide students with sufficient information, colleges should be willing to throw away the theoretically appealing one-to-one advising model if it is found unworkable or experimentally surpassed by use of students, administrators, or other forms of advising.

3

General Education

All general education efforts must be viewed in the context of the growing professionalization of higher education. The university system rewards specialization to such a degree that teaching and interdisciplinary activities are excess baggage, which a professor can safely ignore without endangering his career. A junior professor interested in monetary or professional advancement is not going to get either by becoming a fixture in the Western Civilization course. Accordingly, departments, which now dominate most institutions, view nonmajor teaching and interdisciplinary activities as subversive and are unwilling to supply faculty for general education. When forced to do so by the college administration, departments offer their most junior people, who seek to become disengaged from general education as soon as possible and thereby produce a very high turnover rate in these programs. Furthermore, since faculty are highly trained in only one area, it is difficult for them to teach in interdisciplinary programs. Finally, the high degree of competition and individualistic isolation implied in the current concept of academic freedom make it impossible for faculty to work together in a collaborative fashion. For all these reasons, general education programs are largely unsuccessful and poor in quality.

Core Courses

The core course—the common, broad, interdisciplinary survey required of all students—was studied at Columbia, Eckerd, Reed, and Santa Cruz (Stevenson and Cowell Colleges). Such courses are taught either by common lectures (one or more faculty lecturing to a large class), or by common lectures combined with sections, or by sections alone.

The lone-lecturer, or "great-man," approach has declined in popularity—mainly because of the difficulty involved in finding an instructor who knows the entire area encompassed within the core and is willing to teach it year after year. The Cowell College course (for freshmen) was taught by a single lecturer. This was a required three-quarter course in Western and world civilization—covering Homeric Greece, imperial Rome, and medieval and Renaissance consciousness and culture. In the earliest years of the program, the course was taught by a dynamic instructor who treated the subject matter as his speciality. Following a change in instructors, there was a complete reversal in student and faculty opinion of the course. Faculty who were originally enthusiastic subsequently found the course poor, and students who had been pleased with the course took it only because it was required. The picture that emerges is a course totally dependent in quality upon the one lecturer, almost to the exclusion of the structure and materials.

The faculty team-taught lecture—also combined with sections—was examined at Eckerd, Reed, and Santa Cruz (Stevenson)'. The course at Eckerd (formerly Florida Presbyterian) is a core program spread over the four undergraduate years; students are required to take one course per term. The first two years cover Western civilization, through movies, lectures, and seminars. The third-year course covers Asian, Latin American, and African society, through lectures, discussions, and workshops. The fourth year is devoted to study of the Christian faith, with a weekly lecture and at least one discussion section. The Reed core course, entitled Introduction to Modern Humanities, is a two-year course (the first year required, the second optional) in ancient and modern civilization, conducted through lectures and a weekly seminar. The Stevenson College course, Culture and Society, is a one-quarter course (required of all entering freshmen) on a topic related to the general theme of the individual and society.

The team-taught lecture in general suffers commonly from a lack of cohesion. In this format, faculty from several divisions are brought into the course to give a small number of lectures. At two of the three schools, students found the lectures poor. A majority of participating faculty indicated that they attended none or few of the other faculty lectures. The larger the group of participating faculty, the greater the difficulty in integrating lectures. The more faculty participating, the less the amount of time any individual must put into the course and the greater the feeling of uninvolvement with the program. As a result, there is less faculty willingness to give time to organize the program. Furthermore, since faculty do not receive release time or recognition for giving their one or two lectures, core lecturing becomes a chore. As a result, some faculty members employ the same lecture year after year, despite changes in the core. Similarly, several faculty indicated that they were not used to working with other faculty members. Many faculty said that they could not coordinate their lectures with those in other fields due to their high degree of specialization. Because of these problems, Justin Morrill abandoned a common lecture in its Inquiry and Expression program, a team-taught English-language program, after one year.

Columbia utilizes only core sections for its one-year course (required of all freshmen) in contemporary civilization. The course covers the Reformation, the new science, absolutism and constitutionalism, the Enlightenment, the French Revolution, and the Industrial Revolution. Sections are taught mainly by graduate students, with a few junior faculty and two senior faculty, including the director of the program. Most of the faculty interviewed said that they had been made to teach in the program. Participating faculty are encouraged to leave the core program as quickly as possible, both by the large amount of work involved in core teaching and the need to get back to the department, causing a high turnover rate in core programs. A study of the Columbia Contemporary

Civilization staff from 1935 to 1961, omitting the war years, showed that at no time did the course have more than four faculty who had participated for more than five years. As far back as 1938, there was only one faculty member with more than four years' experience. In all of the years analyzed except three, more than 50 percent of the faculty teaching were new.

Eckerd has allieviated some of these problems by making the four-year core a central part of the curriculum. Accordingly, the necessity to participate in the core program is an obligation explained to all prospective faculty. Professors are expected to participate two out of every three years. The Eckerd core was originally conceived as a way of creating a more cohesive faculty, with at least broad backgrounds if not interdisciplinary tendencies. Faculty participation has been excellent, although some faculty have scoffed at the program.

The lecture-section model used at Eckerd, Reed, Stevenson, and Cowell adds a small-group meeting to the common lecture, much like the addition of a sidecar to a motorcycle—with the essential difference that the sidecar follows the motorcycle. At each of these schools there was sharp criticism, especially by students, of the lack of cohesion between lectures and sections. The discontinuity, which is most apparent between different sections, arises from the narrow disciplinary groundings of the participating faculty. Many, if not most, faculty rely upon their discipline for the orientation of their section. Faculty readily admitted that they emphasize the materials they know and gloss over those that are alien. Furthermore, a number of faculty indicated that in their first year of teaching the core course they were really lost because of the overwhelming amount of new material. Science faculty at Eckerd felt especially helpless. Eckerd realized that this situation was inevitable, and in 1971–1972 began permitting students to choose their section leaders. In addition, Eckerd and Reed hold regular staff meetings to discuss the course material and general course policy, thereby ensuring some level of cohesion within the program. Attendance at such core meetings, however, is usually poor.

The individual-section method used at Columbia motorizes the sidecar and abandons the motorcycle. The commonality of the lectures is transferred to a commonality of materials studied in the sections. A common list of readings is prepared for the course, and each instructor must select at least two of the works on the list for each of the Contemporary Civilization topics, in addition to any other reading desired. Time allocated to each topic and supplementary mimeographed selections are the same throughout the course. This method, however, sacrifices the commonality of learning once used to bring the freshman class together. The sections are very diverse since the participating instructors are drawn from different departments. One instructor likened the sections to introductory courses from each department.

The section format is very costly, especially when section leaders are faculty, as in the programs at Reed, Eckerd, Cowell, and Stevenson. In each program, the core course counts as a regular part of the faculty member's load, so that there is a loss of one course for each section mounted. Since sections are intended as discussion groups, they are small—necessitating a net loss of total student enrollments per faculty member. Columbia reduced the cost by employing graduate students instead of faculty. The core-course load there is usually so heavy that graduate instructors have a poor record of dissertation completions. In addition, graduate students have not been as successful as faculty in teaching. Columbia's *Student Course Evaluation* (1969–1970) rated them below the university norm in clarity, speaking style, and lecture interest.

Most faculty, whether positive or negative to the idea of the core, admitted that they had learned an enormous amount while participating. In fact, many felt they got more out of their course than their students had. However, many students and faculty characterized the core as too ambitious, indicating that the reading is so voluminous that only a superficial treatment of the material is possible. In addition, faculty commonly complained that the cores do not include the natural sciences. A few individuals criticized the core simply for being required. Many more criticized the frequent changes in the core. One faculty member at Eckerd, where change is most common, echoed the group sentiments in saying, "It is always like preparing a new course." Students complained of the uncertainty as to what would be studied in the core.

Interest in cores commonly revives with the creation of new colleges. Prescott and New College both began with required cores, and both programs utterly collapsed due to the difficulties in integrating disciplines and organizing the program, the increased faculty time consumed, and the lack of student interest. Bard attempted a voluntary core in 1970–1971, but this was abandoned for the same reasons as the others, as well as the large expense in using so much faculty time. Similarly, three of the five sample core programs have undergone reduction in requirements. Reed and Columbia had two-year required programs. Reed made the second year optional, while Columbia turned the second year over to the departments providing the core faculty. Most of the second-year courses soon became departmental introductions required for majors by the sponsoring department, and in 1970 the second-year requirement was eliminated. Stevenson College (at Santa Cruz) originally required a three-quarter core, but this requirement was quickly reduced to one quarter.

Distribution Requirements

Core distribution programs consist of heavily prescribed and student-selected courses created for general education purposes, theoretically with a built-in level of coherence; in contrast, smorgasbord distribution programs specify no particular subjects but only general areas of study. Core distribution programs were examined at Residential College of the University of Michigan and Justin Morrill College of Michigan State University. At the time of our study the Residential College's distribution requirements included the freshman seminar; a foreign language (through reading level); three natural science, three social science, and three humanities courses (two courses in each area to be taken in one department); and a course in logic and language. Justin Morrill specified courses in history, religion, philosophy, fine arts, and interdisciplinary humanities (the student could choose any four of these subjects); in politics, psychology, sociology, economics, anthropology, and interdisciplinary social science (the student was required to take twenty credits, no more than two courses or two credits in one area); any natural science courses (twenty credits' worth); a foreign language; courses in aesthetics and expository writing; a time block devoted to field, foreign, or independent study; and a senior seminar.

Faculty and, to a lesser degree, students at both colleges were unsatisfied with their cores and wanted large core changes (Moore, 1970; Francis, 1970). Majorities at both schools thought that the core, as a central part of the curriculum, should be required but that wide flexibility of course selection and sequences is necessary. Some thought that the number of requirements should be reduced, that programs should be more effective in meeting general education objectives, and that the courses should be better organized and coordinated. Students frequently recommended inclusion of more mathematics and science as well as non-Western studies and the performing arts. The language requirement was considered much too extensive and was specifically suggested for deletion. Since the completion of this study, both Justin Morrill and the Residential College have reduced their requirements while still maintaining the core concept. Continual gradual reduction was commonly observed with the result that colleges unwittingly moved from a core to a smorgasbord distribution. Eleven years of such gradual change at Eckerd resulted in a radically different educational experience for its students (see Table 2).

Of all distribution requirements, foreign languages have undergone the least change, due largely to the existence of large

Table 2. ACADEMIC REQUIREMENTS AT ECKERD, 1960–1972

	1960–1961	1962–1963	1966–1967	1968–1969	1971–1972
	Years Required				
Core	4	4	4	4	4
Language	3	3	3	3	dropped
Mathematics	1	1	1	dropped	
Science	1	1	2	dropped	
Social Science	1	dropped			
World Literature	1	dropped			
Number of Courses Required to Graduate	(39)	(36)	(36)	(32)	(32)

departments with tenured professors and the fear that student enrollments will slip sharply. Such fears were not realized at Brown, where language faculty subsequent to the requirement elimination expanded their undergraduate program to include large numbers of offerings in the university freshman-seminar program and lower-division courses of literature in translation. However, Trinity had mixed results, with a sharp decrease in enrollments during the first year after the elimination of the requirement and subsequent small increases in all language departments except French and Greek, which continued to decrease, and Russian, which increased enrollments the first year and maintained this level the second.

The distribution programs at Antioch, Bard, Prescott, Sarah Lawrence, and Santa Cruz can be considered together. Unlike the Residential College and Justin Morrill core distributions, these programs specify only general areas of study. Antioch's requirements include courses in the arts and humanities, physical science, social science, and physical education; in addition, students must pass an examination in English and mathematics skills. Santa Cruz requires three courses in each of three divisions; Bard similarly requires two courses in each of its major divisions, as well as a designated English course. Sarah Lawrence has no specific distribution requirements but specifies a limit of one course per department during a student's first two years.

Student reaction to these programs was largely indifference. Few students at any school felt that the distribution forced them to take courses they ordinarily would not have taken. On the other hand, students praised the quality of the liberal arts experience achieved. Faculty viewed the distribution by comparison with their own general education philosophies rather than through their experience with the program. As a result, faculty replies gave little insight into the actual workings of a distribution program.

Stevenson College at Santa Cruz has completed the only study, among sample schools, of the distribution of graduated students. According to this study, humanities majors graduating in 1970 took an average of 6.85 courses in the social sciences and 2.71 courses in the natural sciences; social science majors took 12.65 humanities and 3.78 natural science courses; natural science majors took 10.8 humanities and 5.08 social science courses. Three courses from each division are required of nonmajors. The study concludes, "If the intention of the campus-wide breadth requirements in humanities, natural sciences, and social sciences is merely to ensure that very student is exposed to at least three courses in each area, then the experience of Stevenson's four-year graduates in 1969–70 would seem to indicate that no regulation is needed to ensure the objective except [for] students majoring in the humanities and social sciences, who are unlikely to take three courses in natural sciences voluntarily" (Wilson, 1971). This result is consistent with interviews conducted among Sarah Lawrence students; 50 percent said that they did not plan to take natural science courses. It should also be noted that students at Santa Cruz are placing a heavy emphasis upon major division, with humanities concentrators taking 26.44 humanities courses (73 percent of their courses), natural science students taking 20.12 natural science courses, and social science students taking 19.57 social science courses.

Instead of outright distribution requirements, Trinity and Haverford prescribe certain guidelines mirroring the typical core distribution program. Students at both schools had no interest in the guidelines, and almost no one indicated using them at all. However, a majority of students at both schools said that they distributed themselves well over the entire curriculum. Others noted omission of one or more areas, commonly including the natural sciences. A number of Trinity students said that they had decided to attend Trinity because they interpreted the guidelines to mean that Trinity had no requirements. In short, the failure of guidelines at Haverford and Trinity has created a de facto free elective system. A small number of the Haverford sample, consisting of only freshmen and sophomores, and a larger number of Trinity students said that they were not distributing because they were already doing major work. The major, particularly at Trinity, serves as a clear demarcation point: most students who have a major are no longer distributing their courses, while those students who are still uncertain about a major distribute because it is the way to find a major. It is likely, based upon interview responses, that students are spending less time on distribution and more time upon the major than in the past; however, it is still too early to examine the difference in distribution patterns occurring before and after the initiation of guidelines.

In 1968–1969 all distribution requirements at New College were eliminated. Students and faculty, with rare exception, were satisfied with the resulting free elective system. A study of diversification for 1969–1970 produced the following results: 6 percent of the students did no work in humanities, 37 percent did no work in the social sciences; and 57 percent did no work in the natural sciences. Moreover, 35 percent of the students did at least 75 percent of their academic work in humanities, 8 percent did at least 75 percent of their work in social science, and 9.4 percent did at least 75 percent of their work in natural science. Even more striking, 24 percent of the students did at least 90 percent of their academic work in humanities, 3.2 percent in social science, and 2 percent in natural science.

A very poor level of distribution is apparent; nonscientists tend not to take science courses, and a sizable number of humanities students take little more than humanities. Students interviewed at Brown, where there is no distribution requirement, also indicated an unwillingness to enroll in science courses.

The findings at Brown, New College, Santa Cruz, Sarah Lawrence, and Trinity indicate that nonscience majors do not voluntarily take science courses. As a result, a school which deems it necessary for students to undertake a given distribution should require that distribution.

Freshman Seminar

The freshman seminar is today the most popular, fastest-growing structure in freshman education. When Harvard adopted them in 1963, the seminars were to provide an opportunity for outstanding freshmen to meet for a semester with Harvard's greatest minds. The program changed rapidly, however, through the inclusion of a cross section of Harvard students and faculty. The elitist rationale was exchanged for the banner under which all freshman-seminar programs now fly: to provide an opportunity for freshmen to work with a faculty member on a topic of mutual interest in a small group. Freshman-seminar programs were studied at Brown, Harvard, Haverford, Sarah Lawrence, Stanford, and Trinity.

Reactions. Faculty and student opinion of the seminars in which they participated was generally positive. A large majority of the faculty at the six schools were positive regarding seminars in which they had participated, and between a plurality and a majority of students were satisfied with their seminars. Students (particularly at the larger schools) appreciated the small size of the seminars and the opportunities provided to work with and know a professor and to meet other freshmen. However, no more than 60 percent of the students at any school felt the freshman seminar program especially appropriate to freshmen. A significant number, often equal in size to the group feeling that seminars are appropriate for freshman year, thought seminars could be useful during any year. Faculty praised seminars primarily for serving as a change of pace and also for permitting more flexibility than regular courses. Many faculty used the course as a laboratory for experimenting with new instructional formats, and several brought these new teaching methods back to their departmental classrooms. Others, however, became disturbed because they could not successfully apply the teaching method perceived as necessary. Additional experience with the seminar will be necessary for some faculty to feel comfortable in the program.

Four significant problems were mentioned in all or most of the programs: the course is above the freshman level; the instructor is not conducting a seminar but only a lecture course; the course lacks content; and freshmen are often too shy to participate fully.

Format. In spite of this apparent consistency in opinions about the seminars, there is really no level of coherence within the program. All that seminars have in common is a course limit (most commonly twelve to fifteen) and certain inbuilt structures, such as advising (at Haverford, Sarah Lawrence, and Trinity) or, at Haverford, a common meeting time to avoid student selections upon time criteria or, at Stanford, the common practice of meeting in the professor's home. In addition, courses are graded either pass/fail or by written evaluation. Only at Stanford (and occasionally at Trinity) are letter grades given.

Course meetings are generally held either once a week for a large block of time or a number of times a week for shorter duration. Only at Trinity did any number of students express a preference for any time format, favoring multiple short meetings. At Harvard seminars usually include work on a project, often done in a professor's laboratory and with his facilities. Other than these givens, the seminar format is completely at the discretion of the instructor.

A different type of format, an open seminar, had been attempted at several schools—notably at Trinity, where the practice was institutionalized. Open seminars are those with no prearranged topic; rather, the students and faculty member together structure the course. In our interviews all but one of the Trinity faculty who had taught open seminars said that they wanted to structure their seminars the next time around—mainly because that is clearly what the students want. A few faculty said that it took the class too long —sometimes as long as three weeks—to choose a topic for the course; and then it became difficult to get appropriate reading materials without even further time loss. As a result of these problems, Trinity's seminars gradually became structured, and by 1972 all seminars had specified topics and format.

Enrollment. Three different enrollment patterns exist in the six programs: required seminar program at Haverford and Sarah Lawrence; recommended nonrequired program at Brown and Trinity; and supplementary program for select freshmen at Harvard and Stanford. The required and recommended programs utilize the seminar as the core of the general education program, and none of those four colleges impose additional general education requirements, though Trinity and Haverford have voluntary general education guidelines. Only at Brown are students other than freshmen admitted into the seminars. According to the registrar, however, only a very small number of sophomores register, so that their impact upon the program is negligible.

In the recommended programs an attempt was made by Trinity and Brown administrators to publicize the programs to obtain high freshman enrollments. In both instances, the effect was an overselling of the program; that is, attributing excessive virtues to the seminars. As a result, the seminars at those two schools were viewed as least successful by their students. Interesting forms of behavior, resulting from salesmanship of seminar programs, were noted. Students would commonly respond, "My seminar was awful, but it's an exception. The program is really excellent." If salesmanship of seminar programs continues, an ever increasing sales pressure will be required to overcome the growing student disillusionment resulting from the continually greater discrepancy between the actual seminar and the advertised product.

The supplementary seminars, more at Harvard than Stanford, serve as an addendum to the freshman program rather than the central feature of the general education program as at other schools. Both Stanford and Harvard have required distributions for general education purposes. At both schools the seminars are oversubscribed, and at Stanford attempts are being made to increase the number of seminars, as noted by the accommodation of three hundred more students in 1970–1971 than in 1969–1970. At Harvard most of the freshmen apply for these seminars, and about 45 percent are selected.

Student Selection. Trinity, Harvard, and Stanford send the entering freshman a description of the individual seminars during the summer prior to freshman registration. The students at Harvard are permitted unlimited seminar choices, at Stanford five choices, and at Trinity three choices. Trinity and Stanford place the student in one of his choices; Harvard gives the student applications to the individual instructors, who choose their own students. Oversubscription is handled at Harvard by screening and at Stanford largely by random selection. At Haverford and Brown students receive seminar descriptions during orientation, and enrollment is on a first-come first-served basis during registration. Sarah Lawrence places students in seminars based upon interest areas indicated in admissions applications.

Each of the selection methods has created serious problems. Placement by student preference has resulted in third-choice placements, which often lead to student dissatisfaction. The lack of flexibility in the number of seminars has made transfer into different seminars for extremely ill-placed students impossible. The problem is far more serious at Trinity than at Stanford because of the more central position of the seminar in the Trinity freshman curriculum. In fact, 15 percent of all students at Trinity were unable to gain admission to any of their three preferences. The first-come first-served method, again, in view of the lack of seminar options, means that a student who is not among the first to register will often be unable to find any seminar of interest. A third of the Brown freshmen interviewed who did not take seminars cited this reason. The process of screening students by the seminar instructors at Harvard has caused great unhappiness and feelings of inadequacies for rejected applicants, despite the fact that most instructors admitted a degree of arbitrariness in their choices. A few professors each year find the selection of students so difficult that they admit a few more than the limit of fifteen, which is undesirable for small-group interaction.

A subsidiary problem, according to faculty and students, is that at the time of enrollment students frequently do not know well enough what the seminar will study, how the seminar will operate, or what the instructor is like. At Brown, therefore, it was proposed that the Modes of Thought courses (freshman seminars) begin one or two weeks after the other courses, so that the students could investigate possible courses more fully before deciding on one, or even that all Modes of Thought courses be deferred until second semester. Deferring seminars until second semester would be deleterious to any advising function of the seminars. On the other hand, instead of beginning classes two weeks late, Haverford and Brown provide occasions for students to meet seminar leaders and discuss their courses during orientation week. Unfortunately, such meetings have been poorly attended by faculty and students. Perhaps, however, additional features such as trial seminars with seminar instructors, during orientation, fuller descriptions of seminars and of seminar leaders' expectations, and increased opportunities for prospective students to meet seminar instructors during orientation period might provide the information needed. These measures, however, will work only if they have the cooperation of freshmen and faculty instructors.

Instructors. The Brown, Harvard, Haverford, Sarah Lawrence, and Trinity programs all rely principally upon college or university faculty, though senior faculty make up a minority of program staffs. At Stanford resource people outside the faculty are used in addition to the faculty.

Brown obtains additional staff from the graduate student ranks. In 1969–1970 about 10 percent of the teaching staff were graduate assistants; by 1972–1973 that figure had risen to 33 percent. However, graduate students probably should not be added to a freshman-seminar program unless the program staff definitely agree that the quality of the program will not be affected. If it is decided that the effect will not be negative, then graduate students, who are very cheap instructors, should be employed liberally, provided they meet the program's specifications, in order to expand the seminar offerings to a workable number.

Trinity occasionally uses undergraduate teaching assistants in seminars. The program director and the two faculty interviewed at Trinity who had worked with the teaching assistants indicated that these students cut down the distance between faculty and freshmen. At Brown, one faculty member used two undergraduate assistants with the same result. Several Trinity faculty felt the assistants had been so successful that they planned to employ one in their next seminar. Graduate teaching assistants were not as successful, since freshmen perceived them as closer in role to the professor than themselves. The addition of undergraduate teaching assistants might be a useful tool in diminishing freshmen shyness manifest in a lack of participation in seminars. Trinity provided teaching assistants with the incentive of one course credit for their participation in the seminar.

About a third of the seminar staff at Stanford are from areas that do not teach undergraduates. This method of faculty employment brings to the seminars those faculty with lighter teaching loads, who are more likely to be able to teach freshman seminars without having to drop other course responsibilities. This is an economical way of increasing seminar offerings and providing added perspectives to the program. Furthermore, the use of graduate and professional faculty also provides input at the graduate level as to the condition of undergraduate education. One quarter of the entire Stanford faculty sample indicated the seminar was their first experience teaching undergraduates and that they were grateful for the experience. The success of these instructors presents many similar possibilities for economical expansion of freshman-seminar programs —for instance, through the use of volunteer retired faculty, community professionals, and others.

According to program administrators at each school, all participating faculty are volunteers. When the number of volunteers is insufficient, an administrative headhunter is sent to negotiate with departments to free people who want to teach. Yet over one fifth of the Trinity faculty and others from Brown and Haverford complained about being forced to participate in the program.

A problem of all freshman-seminar programs has been the faculty's lack of interest, especially in rigidly departmentalized colleges and graduate-oriented universities. The Brown freshman-seminar committee was forced to use exceptional flexibility in approval of seminar proposals owing to the "disappointingly small number of proposals submitted." In Trinity's 1969–1970 program evaluation, Director Richard Lee indicated difficulty in "persuading the best men we have to donate a large part of their energy to this kind of teaching" in that "it does not typically increase one's paycheck or professional standing." Trinity's 1970–1971 freshman-seminar director, Borden Painter, said that departments often provide fewer faculty than requested and feel that they are doing the program a favor.

The reasons expressed by faculty for their nonparticipation in the seminar program offer no cause to feel hopeful. A majority of nonparticipants indicated greater interest in their department or field and lack of interest in the seminar program. Professors at Brown echoed the sentiments of the faculty leader who said, "Interdisciplinary programs of any sort, which were encouraged under the new curriculum, receive no help at all or are sabatoged by departments. What you're doing in effect is asking any individual [who participates] to cut off his ties to the life blood of his career."

Funding. Brown, Haverford, Sarah Lawrence, and Trinity do not fund their freshman-seminar programs. The nonfunding creates severe problems in faculty staffing. The distribution of seminars at Brown is therefore badly unbalanced. In 1969–1970 Brown had twenty-one science, twenty-two humanities, and four social science seminars; in 1970–1971, twenty-four science, forty-one humanities, and ten social science seminars. Haverford had eight science, thirty-five humanities, and eleven social science seminars in 1970–1971. Another manifestation of staffing difficulties is the inability of programs to provide adequate numbers of seminars. Trinity, for instance, was able to mount only thirty-six of thirty-nine desired seminars.

At Brown the participating departments are the larger ones with the lightest teaching loads; some of the smaller departments with heavier loads provide no freshman-seminar faculty. To illustrate the problem more graphically, engineering and biology medical science, the departments with the greatest numbers of faculty, rated sixth and seventh in the number of undergraduates enrolled; while sociology/anthropology and history rated sixth and eleventh in faculty size and second and fourth in the number of undergraduates enrolled. As a result, small departments with heavier teaching loads are unable to release faculty for seminar teaching. A faculty member desiring to teach a seminar must therefore do so in addition to his regular teaching load, though this is even the practice in a number of larger departments. Several individuals at Trinity also taught seminars in addition to their regular course load, although the freshman-seminar committee at Brown indicated some improvement in this area. Nevertheless, for the junior instructor, teaching a seminar means increasing his teaching load, cutting his research time, and ultimately being denied tenure. Aside from the fact that junior people will not participate under these conditions, the impact upon the freshman-seminar program would be a lack of continuity, since all faculty who participated in the program would be forced to leave the school. One junior faculty member indicated that he was willing to work under these conditions. He went to his department chairman to ask permission to teach a seminar above his load; the chairman denied the request, explaining that, if the department permitted such activity, the administration would expect it in the future.

Regardless of whether departments or individual faculty are granted stipends, it is absolutely necessary to establish a program budget. At Brown, which has no such budget, many faculty complained that their class expenses must come from their own pockets, research money, or the department's budget. Similarly, at Stanford, which encourages informal meetings at the professor's home, one faculty member complained about having to pay for food and drink for his class each week. Forcing instructors to pay such costs is undoubtedly injurious to staff morale.

Stanford and Harvard do fund their freshman-seminar programs, at very high cost. Harvard provides no remuneration for senior participating faculty; junior faculty are given a decrease in course load, for which the program must reimburse the appropriate department. Payments for release time account for $78,000 of the program's $100,000 budget. For the first three years of the Stanford program, the only compensation offered was a graduate assistant for senior faculty and the possibility of release time for junior faculty. Participating graduate students received one-quarter teaching appointments. Since 1968 provision has been made in the program's $79,000 budget to pay most seminar instructors. It should be noted that Stanford staffs nearly twice as many seminars as Harvard at a lesser cost.

Funding of seminars creates as many problems as nonfunding in that it then becomes increasingly difficult to obtain a program faculty willing to participate without funding. Departments are unwilling to let junior people, even with light teaching loads, participate without repayment for their slots. As a result of this financial limitation, Harvard and Stanford are both unable to mount sufficient seminars to accommodate their entire freshman classes.

Tufts avoided the funding problem by organizing an ad hoc seminar program. The Experimental College offers a voluntary program of seminars for freshmen, limited to enrollments of twelve. After freshman registration, if seminars are not full, upperclassmen are permitted to enroll. All the seminars are taught by undergraduates, and instructors receive course credit for their participation. The program has been popular: "Those who have participated, either as students or leaders, usually strongly endorse the freshman-seminar program. . . . Peer teaching may have special values in such a setting, exposing the freshman to one teacher who is of his own generation and yet is more experienced and knowledgeable" (Trefethen, 1970). Limitations in peer teaching are serious, however. Students at Tufts reported putting less work into peer-taught courses than faculty-led courses. The program also offers significant advantages, including a lack of cost for the entire program and accommodations for all interested members of the Tufts freshman class. However, enrollments and numbers of courses mounted have been somewhat erratic. The major problem, aside from those difficulties found inherent in peer teaching, is that the Tufts program runs contrary to many of the rationales for initiating a freshman-seminar program. (For a full discussion of peer teaching, see Chapter Seven.)

Special Programs

The programs considered in this cluster are the Yale Directed Studies program, the Berkeley Experimental College Program, and the St. John's four-year program. All of these programs are similar in that they are intended for a self-selected group of students to utilize a core format consuming all or part of the participant's time. As a result of the self-selection, these programs were generally popular with the participating students and faculty—more universally popular than any other core program discussed. The three programs represent a continuum from which to examine faculty roles and structures in higher education. The Yale program is assembled on a departmental basis—with all the attendant problems of division of material into departmental boxes, lack of coordination in content and effort by participating departments, and forced participation of junior faculty. The Experimental College Program at Berkeley had a uniform nondepartmentalized curriculum and a self-selected full-time faculty; however, because the faculty still adhered to the university's traditional reward system, they were unable to work together, and most attempts at cooperative planning failed completely. St. John's College has avoided the practices of Yale and the Experimental College Program because of a difference in values. The curriculum is not divided, and there are no rewards for specialization; rather, each faculty member is required to prepare himself to teach the entire curriculum. Similarly, faculty members are encouraged to audit each other's classes—an abandonment of the concept of academic freedom, which is commonly construed to bar faculty from each other's classes. As a result, St. John's has succeeded in creating the best functioning of the three general education programs.

Directed Studies. Directed Studies is a freshman and sophomore general education program admitting only a select group of Yale freshmen. The program is unashamedly elitist and aims to accept only those students who have shown most academic promise. Students are given the opportunity to apply after acceptance by

Yale. Approximately 220 students apply each year (slightly less than 20 percent of the freshman class), and between seventy and ninety-five are admitted. College Board scores are the crucial factor in admission to Directed Studies; students with scores below 750 are rarely accepted. Students completing one year have the option of continuing for a second, and about two thirds of the students do so. The program employs twenty-four faculty members and is run with its own budget. Only five of the twenty-four professors teaching Directed Studies in 1970–1971 were still in the program in 1972–1973. In most cases, participation in Directed Studies counts as part of the instructor's regular course load.

The Directed Studies courses are specifically designed for the program and are taken only by Directed Studies students. In the freshman year, courses are offered in literature, philosophy, history of art, history and politics, mathematics, and biology. Students planning to concentrate in the humanities take the first four courses, with the option of substituting a language course and either mathematics or biology. Students planning to major in the sciences take three of the first four courses and may select any two science courses in the university, including the two Directed Studies courses. The second year focuses on the social sciences; courses are offered in economics, law and society, literature, philosophy, religious studies (eliminated in 1972–1973), and sociology. Each of these fields is presented through topics considerably more narrow than the courses offered the first year. The courses, particularly in the first year, are taught with lectures and sections; but the emphasis is on the sections, which usually account for two of the three hours of weekly meetings. The program director indicated that Directed Studies in recent years has become more specialized, which has hurt the program by fostering less of a feeling of common interest among the students in it.

Faculty members interviewed approved of certain features of the program—the ability of the students, the small classes, the teaching flexibility and freedom. The weaknesses pointed out, however, are significant and indicate that the program might be in serious need of rethinking. Elitism, the program's greatest strength, is also its greatest weakness. Nearly half of the faculty felt that the program is designed for the wrong people; it "encourages verbal kids to talk too much" while leaving the nonverbal students in big lectures. Lack of coordination in the program was another commonly mentioned weakness. It was felt that each department works too independently, thus providing little integration in the program. Recently, fewer faculty were volunteering to teach Directed Studies, so that the staff was being dominated by new and younger drafted teachers.

The director and the *Course Critique* felt that most students in Directed Studies like the program. The *Course Critique* pointed out several strengths and weaknesses of the program. The strengths are that students and their work receive greater faculty attention, a sense of community results from common class membership, and the survey courses are better than those in the regular curriculum. The major weakness is the lack of an integrated approach. The lack of common backgrounds for students in the courses exacerbates this problem. Directed Studies, according to the *Course Critique,* is a poor program for students who dislike further writing, are sure of their major, or are introverted in class. Nevertheless, it is highly likely that these are the students who would benefit most from Directed Studies.

Experimental College Program. The first two-year cycle of the Berkeley Experimental College Program began in September 1965. (After two such cycles, 1965–1967 and 1967–1969, the program was at least temporarily discontinued.) A description of the program was sent to all Berkeley freshmen with an invitation to join. Applications were received from 325 of the 4800 freshman (mainly students who planned to concentrate in humanities or social sciences), and 150 students were randomly chosen. Students were required to take one course per semester outside the program, with two thirds to three quarters of their academic load taken in the Experimental College.

The curriculum was divided into four periods: Greece, seventeenth-century England, the American constitutional founding, and the contemporary scene. It had a theme or problem orientation, exploring freedom and authority, individual and society, war and peace, conscience and the law, and acceptance and rebellion. The periods were used as historical clusterings (cultures) through which to examine the themes. The program material centered around a short, common, great books and documents reading list. A course calendar, listing readings and illustrating curricular division, is available in *Experiment at Berkeley* (Tussman, 1969).

Instead of the usual course-building unit, the program was broken down into lectures, seminars, and conferences. Lectures were scheduled twice a week for about an hour and a half each, and all students and faculty were expected to attend. Though the lectures were coordinated with the reading, lecturers did not discuss what was read or give glosses; rather, they tried to raise questions and examine problems by employing the literature. Lecture formats varied from a single faculty lecturer, either from within or from outside the program, to a group presentation by some or all of the participating faculty. The only uniform feature of the lectures was that all ended with a question-and-answer period.

The lectures received the least enthusiastic comment of any feature embodied in the program. Students said that there was too much bickering among lecturers, an opinion corroborated by Tussman (1969): "With some exceptions Tuesdays [lectures] fell apart . . . when deliciously real faculty quarrels boiled over into public view. The staff was generally upset and worried . . . and students [were] frequently disappointed." Only one student in the sample praised the lectures, and faculty conspicuously omitted discussion of them. Despite the depth of criticism, Joseph Tussman, the initiator and director of the program, considered the lectures a necessary unifying experience in a common learning program.

Seminars went through much change in the two cycles of the program, starting with groups of thirty students meeting one afternoon a week and ending with groups of eight students meeting twice a week, once alone and once with an instructor. The structure of each seminar was left to the discretion of its instructor. Enthusiasm for the seminar structure was great. One third of the students and faculty characterized the seminar as a principal strength of the program. The student-led seminar was disappointing, however, because of poor attendance and inability of the seminar to make progress without a faculty leader.

Writing was viewed as an essential part of the program, and each student was expected to spend at least an hour a day writing. For this purpose, students were asked to maintain a journal, which would be examined periodically. In addition, five formal papers were assigned per semester with specified form and topic. Initially a term project was also required, but this requirement was abandoned. Conferences were held every two weeks for each student to examine his writing. Students and faculty both praised these conferences.

In the first cycle, five Berkeley faculty were hired, two from speech, one from aeronautic engineering, one from philosophy, and one from political science. After one year, one faculty member, who had secured only a one-year leave, left the program as did another who was dissatisfied. In the second cycle, six faculty were involved, and all completed the program. The first-cycle faculty was recruited by Tussman from Berkeley faculty acquaintances who had expressed interest in teaching the program. The second group consisted of friends chosen by Tussman from outside the Berkeley campus.

According to a study of the first cycle of the program (Suczek and Alfert, 1971), faculty could agree only that they wanted to take part in the program. They did not have what at least one faculty member considered essential: "a shared vision of the aim of education." Although faculty readily admitted disharmony in the program, most of them praised the advantages of working with an interdisciplinary group. They did complain that the program demanded an excessive time commitment. It was clearly impossible to continue with research or outside activities, and common suggestions were that one in every three or four years be spent outside the program. All faculty, however, even one who had bitterly attacked Tussman, praised the conception of the program. In fact, a few students and faculty thought that this was the best lower-division program in America. Two thirds of the faculty called the program a great teaching experience, and several faculty talked of taking part in or initiating such a program elsewhere; one faculty member actually did so at the University of British Columbia.

An important feature in the Experimental College Program was the political emphasis. This feature was criticized by nearly half of the students and commented upon by most of the faculty. Tussman's bias in the program was that students could be given a sense of freedom by being taught the obligations of good citizenship, and this orientation differed from that of other faculty. Several of the faculty and students referred to the program's process as "Tuss-manizing." One student in particular talked of a cathartic experience in realizing that he no longer thought about things, but rather applied a "Tussmanized" standard. Nonetheless, there appeared to be a great deal of intellectual freedom for students in the program. According to Suczek (1972), the first-cycle students—whether they liked or disliked or were indifferent to the program—all perceived the program as offering great freedom.

Attrition was a significant problem in the program. About 40 percent of the students in the Experimental College left the program, the same as the percentage of students in the regular Berkeley program who left the university. For the attrition of this philosophically distinct and self-selected program to equal that of the liberal arts college at Berkeley, the process and/or information used for selection of students must have been severely deficient, especially considering the positive responses of those who stayed in the program. (For an interesting study of personality differences between the Experimental College student and other Berkeley students, see Suczek, 1972.)

Those students who did complete the program expressed difficulty in making the transition from the Experimental College to the upper division. Of the ninety students who completed the second cycle, approximately fifteen took their junior year abroad. About half of the students found that they were not prepared for upper-division study (the approach, not the content), and many found disciplinary study lacking in cohesion. As a remedy, a few students suggested that the program's length be increased to four years. Nonetheless, according to a study by Schaaf (1971), Experimental College students had higher grades and made fewer changes in upper-division majors. In addition, 58 percent of the Experimental College students as compared to 48 percent of the regular Berkeley students, received diplomas four years after entering the university.

When one finally appraises this Experimental College program at Berkeley, and duly notes the disharmony and lack of integration, he is forced to take into account the unusual sense of involvement inspired by the program. The people interviewed had been visibly and certainly emotionally affected by their participation in the program. In most other programs observed, disinterested responses by faculty and students were common; however, Experimental College participants leapt at the opportunity to discuss their experiences and spoke paternalistically about the ways the program could be improved, a subject that each interviewee had previously thought about in depth. The feeling of paternalism and proprietorship resulted in many an overzealous comment or an attitude often verging on worship or hatred.

St. John's College. The conventional way of describing a college by breaking it down into departments or by into requirements versus electives or by discussing its general education requirements is not applicable to St. John's. There are no departments; all faculty are simply St. John's tutors. And there are, except for preceptorials (nine weeks in-depth studies), no electives; all students take the same required program, a program of great books—classics from Plato and Homer through Virgil, Dante, and Shakespeare to Melville, Faraday, Freud, and Marx (see Table 3). The list of books varies only slightly from year to year. When asked whether they would like to see the curriculum broadened or narrowed in any way, most students agreed that "you don't mess with something that works."

Students attend a seminar based on books from the program for each of the four years. Seminars, each with fifteen to twenty students and two tutors, meet twice a week for at least two hours. They are started by one of the tutors, who asks a question about that week's reading; a free-flowing discussion follows. This was a chief strength of the program for some students. A weakness mentioned comparatively frequently, however, was the "idle rap." There were complaints that some students did not contribute and that others would try to dominate discussion. Students also have a language and a mathematics tutorial each year, as well as a music tutorial in the sophomore year. In addition, each year groups of fifteen to twenty students meet with a tutor twice a week for science laboratory (studying such topics as theory of measurement, biology, classical mechanics, and atomic theory). The different backgrounds of students, particularly in music and mathematics, have proved to be problems in these tutorials.

Preceptorials, added to the program in 1962, allow a nine-week period in which juniors and seniors, with a tutor, can study one book or theme in depth. The preceptorial replaces the seminar for that period and provides the only place in the curriculum where the student has some choice, since he can choose any of fifteen to twenty preceptorials offered each year. Preceptorials were praised by tutors for permitting a chance to study one area of interest in depth and lessening the classical emphasis of the curriculum. Some tutors felt that more should be offered and that the nine-week period should be lengthened, although all agreed that they should be kept out of the first two years of the program. The students interviewed either liked their preceptorials or were looking forward to them. Those who had already taken theirs mentioned that they provided all the relevance needed in the college and that they were small and "unrushed." (Typical of subjects providing this relevance seemed to be Descartes's *Discourses* and Plato's *Symposium.*)

Another component of the St. John's program is the formal lecture, a Friday-night presentation by an outsider or tutor, followed by a discussion. These are held almost every week and often attract people from surrounding communities as well as students and faculty. This structure received praise from students and faculty alike.

The teaching load at St. John's is unique. The goal of every tutor is to be able to teach the entire program, although there are now only a handful of tutors capable of doing this. It was said that even new tutors can teach the parts of the program they want without having the disappointment common elsewhere of having to "earn" the right to teach the best courses. The average tutor's weekly schedule includes four class hours for the seminar, four class hours for a tutorial, and another four or five hours for an additional tutorial or a laboratory. In addition, he has innumerable informal meetings and up to forty-five paper conferences with individual students each term, sits in on oral examinations and the oral grading session each semester, and serves on the usual faculty committees. Finally, many tutors audit other classes so that they will be able to teach them in following years.

The most common weakness mentioned by tutors is the amount of time consumed by the program. Tutors said that there is simply too much to do, although they were quick to acknowledge

Table 3. THE CURRICULUM AT ST. JOHN'S (1970–1972)

	Literature	Philosophy and Theology	History and Social Science	Mathematics and Natural Science	Music
First Year	Homer	Plato	Herodotus	Euclid*	
	Aeschylus	Aristotle	Thucydides	Nicomachus*	
	Sophocles	Lucretius	Plutarch	Ptolemy*	
	Euripides			Lavoisier*	
	Aristophanes			Dalton*	
Second Year	Virgil	Aristotle	Plutarch	Ptolemy*	Palestrina*
	Dante	Epictetus	Tacitus	Apollonius*	Bach*
	Chaucer	Plotinus	Dante	Galen	Mozart*
	Rabelais	The Bible	Machiavelli	Copernicus*	Beethoven*
	Shakespeare	Augustine	Gibbon	Kepler	Schubert*
	Donne*	Anselm		Harvey*	Verdi
	Marvell*	Thomas Aquinas		Descartes	Stravinsky*
		Luther		Darwin	
		Calvin		Mendel*	
		Montaigne			
		Bacon			

Third Year	Cervantes Milton Swift Racine* Fielding Melville	Descartes Pascal Hobbes Spinoza Locke Berkeley Leibniz Hume Kant	Locke Rousseau Adam Smith U.S. Constitution Hamilton, Madison, Jay Tocqueville	Galileo Kepler Newton* Leibniz Huygens*	Mozart
Fourth Year	Molière* La Fontaine* Goethe Tolstoi Dostoevski Baudelaire* Rimbaud* Valéry* Yeats*	Hegel Kierkegaard Nietzsche William James Peirce	Hegel Marx Documents from American Political History	Faraday* Lobachevski* Dedekind* Maxwell* J. J. Thomson* Bohr* Millikan* Schrödinger* Darwin Freud Einstein*	

* Studied in the tutorials or laboratory.

that shortening the reading list might remove some of their favorites, and lessening the work load is a financial impossibility without weakening the program. Individuals said that there is little time to pursue a line of inquiry, they cannot follow their individual interests, some books are not studied adequately, and the demands on students are too great. Two factors, however, tempered this criticism. First, even from those who protested the skimpy treatment of some works, there was a strong feeling that students should be instilled with an interest in the great books, which will last them all their lives. If the program is successful, the students will go back in future years and study the works in greater depth. Tutors particularly approved the lack of emphasis on disciplines, so that the humanities are not separated from the sciences. Second, as an assistant dean pointed out, the program is flexible, and as a consensus is reached that there is too much material, some works are dropped. Connected with this were the comments of the younger tutors that it is "a frantic existence trying to carry such a load and deal with so much new material."

Accepting a position at St. John's involves a great risk. Because there are less than fifty hours a day, one must devote oneself completely to the program in order to fulfill what is expected. Thus, tutors establish neither a reputation nor contacts in their fields or, for that matter, in any part of the academic world outside St. John's. This, coupled with the fact that 75 percent of the new tutors are denied tenure, would seem to make a teaching position at St. John's as desirable as a hair shirt. Yet hundreds of applications are received each year for the few open teaching positions.

What is important to note is that faculty at St. John's, unlike other college faculties, accept the limitations of their school. For the most part, they would oppose changing the program in any way, even if it meant that their particular complaint could be removed. In addition, despite their criticisms, they do not leave St. John's unless they are forced to. They are very dedicated to the program and willing to accept the risk involved in working at a school which allows them no chance to make a "professional reputation."

Because St. John's accepts students only as freshmen, the student body is weighted toward the early years. Thus, in 1969–

1970 there were 125 freshmen, 97 sophomores, 66 juniors, and 59 seniors. Currently, the admissions office aims for a freshman class of 126, or twenty-one in each of six seminars and fourteen in each of nine tutorials. Faculty consistently praised the students for their high intelligence and commitment to the program.

In 1969–1970 St. John's accepted 69 percent of its applicants, and 74 percent of these enrolled. The high acceptance rate and small enrollment indicate that a large number of applicants regard the school as their first choice. The program was a significant factor in all but one student's decision to come to St. John's. About half mentioned the program by name as the most powerful attracting force, while other students listed reasons closely connected to the program.

Transfer students are an interesting phenomenon at St. John's. The program is viewed as an integrated unit; therefore, all new students, including transfers, start as freshmen. Yet about 20 percent of each year's freshman class consists of transfer students. The four-year matriculation required for transfers causes a peculiar problem. That is, the school cannot compensate for dropouts by accepting a large number of transfer students. The attrition rate is consistently over 50 percent during the four years; that is, less than half of the entering students graduate four years later. Up to one sixth are asked to leave, a larger group transfer to other schools; of the rest, administrators are quick to point out, some come back and finish years later.

From the initiation of the great books program in 1937 until 1967, about 2400 students entered St. John's, and 642 graduated (27 percent). These figures include the Santa Fe campus, open since 1964. Fifty-nine percent of the graduates went to graduate or professional school, and a large percentage of others went into teaching. A study compiled by the alumni office in 1967 shows the distribution of fields for the 380 graduates who, at that time, had attended graduate school. The study indicates a wide diversity in professional fields. Seven alumni are currently tutors at St. John's.

As a general criticism some tutors said that St. John's intellectual withdrawal from the rest of the academic world gives its students and tutors too great a feeling of superiority. One tutor described the present attitude at St. John's as somewhat "monastic";

another said that the faculty devote themselves so totally to the program that they tend to become passive and uncritical. Another felt that the common program itself is a problem because the lack of diversity of tutors' interests makes faculty life somewhat boring. One tutor simply said that the school is a "little too rigid."

Students too pointed to the "incestuous," "ivory tower" nature of the school, and some added that St. John's despises other educational ventures to the extent that it becomes bored with itself and ignores its own problems. Several students complained that St. John's is too small; others said that it is too intense. Another group said that it is a dull place socially, and several others blamed all the college's woes on its being in a town as "boring" as Annapolis.

Among the changes suggested was that St. John's become part of a larger college complex, although the tutor who suggested this was afraid that some of the closeness now present might be lost. Another suggested solution to the same problem was that students be encouraged to work off campus to ease the claustrophobia.

Conclusion

With an increasing technological need for greater specialization, general education is increasingly important to provide a basis for common humanity among people. Specialization isolates people, underlines their differences, and is, in this sense, divisive. General education is capable of providing a commonality sufficient to surmount the differences in vocation.

No program examined, with the possible exception of St. John's, succeeded in providing this type of general education. The failure of general education lies in the division of people and knowledge into discrete containers. At the modern university, prescribing that students take a course in language, a course in science, and a course in history means not that the student obtains a more humane view of life but that the student is taught scholarship from the point of view of a linguist, an historian, and a scientist. Such courses have distinctly created boundaries and relate to each other in no practical way. The type of general education desired is that which seeks to build bridges where these boundaries now lie. One of the atomic scientists who worked on the Manhattan Project said he felt as little responsibility for the bomb as a maker of cans should feel when a can is thrown through a window. Looming even larger than the question of right or wrong is this man's isolation—to such a degree that he was unable to see the next step beyond his atomic theory work. The kind of general education necessary to combat this problem is not necessarily an interdisciplinary course mounted by three departments and taught by five specialists. Even a program administered by a single department can have an inbuilt dimension showing commonality—showing where the field stands with regard to the rest of the world.

This is where general education courses fail. There are few general educationists left. Scholarship forces scholars so far apart that they can no longer understand each other. These people are clearly unable to help their students perceive the breadth of their endeavors. Until this situation is reversed through changes in graduate education and reward systems, general education will remain as it is. Colleges can begin to approach this problem by use of incentives in general education efforts. Encouraging departments to move together instead of further apart is imperative. Universities have reached the point where professors in the same department do not have to associate with one another, as noted by the proliferation of journals of different topics in the same field.

The failure of general education is indicative of the most fundamental problem noted in the study—the inability of people to work together and understand each other. People from various areas must get together and teach each other and, in so doing, guide their students. If they do not, the results will be far more serious than the degeneration of higher education, rather, we stand to lose even the thin threads of humanity that unite us.

Comprehensive Examinations and Senior Year

ᘓᘓᘓᘓᘓᘓᘓᘓᘓᘓᘓᘓᘓᘓᘐᘐᘐᘐᘐᘐᘐᘐᘐᘐᘐᘐ

As students pass through college, they are seldom asked to stop for a moment to put together what they have learned. Most often students take a course here and three there to fill requirements and a major, designed as a coherently structured concentration but too often a disassociated group of courses. As a course ends, a test is taken and passed, the course notebook filed, and the course material forgotten. The specifics of any one course may not be too important, but all of these experiences together should say something. That's the stuff that formal education is, or should be.

Some colleges, in an attempt to make students stop for that moment occasionally, require a comprehensive examination, which has the potential to ask students to put together what they have learned; a senior thesis, which can ask students to apply what they have learned; or a senior seminar, which may help students discover where their major fits into the rest of the world. None of the colleges studied sought to create lifelong analysis skills, but all hoped to add some coherence to their programs by use of these devices.

Comprehensive Examinations

Colleges and universities in many countries avoid issues such as course grading and requirements by making use of various college-wide and, in some cases, nationwide comprehensive examinations. While in the United States some comprehensive tests have certainly become components for the transition from high school to college; and from college to graduate or professional schools, much less use is made of such examinations within the undergraduate years. Hampshire College, in Amherst, Massachusetts, is a notable exception, using examinations instead of grades as the means of passage through the curriculum. Similarly, Sterling College, in Sterling, Kansas, divides its curriculum into nine "competencies," which students can fulfill either by examination or courses and experiences. In addition, quite a few colleges, including several of the schools studied, maintain some form of comprehensive as a supplement to the course grading system. The comprehensives studied have moved away from the traditionally uniform examination to a format that recognizes the student as an individual and minimizes the occurrence and fear of failure. Comprehensive examinations can be defined as written or oral tests administered universally to the members of one academic year. Such examinations were studied at Bard, Haverford, Reed, St. John's, Santa Cruz, and New College—schools representing a spectrum ranging from classical to innovative curricula.

Sophomore examinations. A few schools have felt a need for a rite of passage between the freshman and sophomore years of general education, and the junior and senior years of specialization. Bard College, for example, divides its program into an "upper" and a "lower" college, with a "moderation" examination required for transition. Moderation consists of a student self-assessment through a required paper, other academic tasks (required by some departments), and an oral defense before a faculty board of three from the division in which the student desires to concentrate. The moderation is held during the sophomore year to determine whether the division will accept the student as a major. A student failing moderation must apply to moderate in a different division; he may not choose a different major option within that division. About 10 percent of the students fail moderation on the first attempt.

Bard's faculty were more positive regarding the moderation, at least in theory, than were its students. Most of the faculty praised the concept of providing students with a needed period of introspection, although many felt that the moderation has deteriorated over the years, and at least one division was in the process of re-evaluating it. Only a small number of faculty felt that the examination creates undue anxiety, although several indicated that it is very difficult for transfer students.

Less than one third of Bard's students were happy with the practice of moderation, although, like the faculty, a significant number were enthusiastic about the concept. Similarly, less than one third of those who had already experienced the moderation had found it valuable. The students also pointed out a certain arbitrariness in the use of the examination among different divisions. For example, all the students who had taken the moderation in one division said that it is impossible to fail while all those in another said that the examination is used by their division to cut down its oversubscription. In addition, several students indicated that the ease of moderation depends as much upon who is on the panel as in what division the moderation occurs. One often-expressed fear concerning ordeals such as moderation is that great, and implicitly harmful, anxiety will be created as the students worry about failing. At Bard, 40 percent of the sample, when asked, indicated such feelings.

St. John's College employs a similar procedure, called "sophomore enabling." Sophomore enabling is a review, conducted by the instruction committee, of the student's first two years at the college. As a major part of enabling, all sophomores are required to write an essay summarizing what they have learned. After reviewing the student's essay and his record, the committee then decides whether he should continue at the college. Decisions fall within three categories: the student is "enabled," becoming a junior; or the student is told specific work he must do to be enabled; or the student is not enabled and is asked to leave the college. In 1969–1970 almost one fifth of the sophomores were ultimately not enabled. Most left the college; only a few chose to repeat the sophomore year.

Because St. John's, unlike Bard, requires its students to meet individually with all their professors each term, sophomore enabling was not considered as unique as moderation was at Bard. Nevertheless, faculty and student reactions were not dissimilar—the faculty at St. John's generally positive, the students with very mixed feelings. The anxiety caused by enabling apparently is greater than that encountered at Bard, since many students reported that they had no idea what was being examined, or how to prepare for it, or on what basis judgments were made.

Both St. John's and Bard combine the potentially worthwhile idea of requiring students to examine where they have been and where they are going with the somewhat tired structure of a comprehensive examination, with its judgments of success and failure. Thus, the important issues of what a student learns and what he wants to do with it are made subsidiary to passing. A more successful approach is the freshman evaluation at Haverford College (see Chapter Two), which could be used with sophomores. At the end of the freshman year, each student meets with a panel of faculty and seniors to discuss the student's general education program and future plans. The panel is charged with making advisory recommendations for the student, including further studies if necessary.

Until recently, New College required all sophomore students to take a qualifying examination to enter each department as a major. Because each department treated the examination differently, this requirement was dropped in 1970, and the examination was left as an option to each department. Only two departments, biology and mathematics, chose to continue it.

Junior examinations. Reed College imposes a junior qualifying examination to ascertain each student's ability to write the required senior thesis. A student is given two chances to pass this examination; if he fails both times, he is denied the opportunity to continue in that department. After a student has failed once, however, some departments now go over his weaknesses with him and tutor him for several weeks until he can pass the second time. Perhaps as a result of these efforts, the failure rate has been drastically reduced. The registrar reported a past failure rate of 15 percent and a current failure rate of 3 percent or 4 percent.

Like most of the examinations mentioned, Reed's aroused little enthusiasm from students and only theoretical praise from instructors. The faculty were divided largely between those who felt that the examination has symbolic value as a final barrier and those who thought it a meaningless ritual; only a small number considered it a useful review of the first three years. The students were not particularly disturbed or anxious about the examination, but neither did they consider it especially beneficial. Many of them, however, agreed that the idea of reviewing their progress after three years was probably a good one.

Senior-year examinations. Some colleges (in our study Reed, New College, and Santa Cruz) require a comprehensive examination in the senior year. At Reed, graduating seniors are required to take a two-hour oral examination based on their entire college experience but focusing on the thesis and the senior-year work. According to Reed's registrar, no one has failed this examination in many years, and it has become only a psychological hurdle.

New College requires a senior examination called the baccalaureate, which is administered by a committee of the student's professors, two other students, and the senior-project advisor. The purpose of this examination is generally to review each student's work and senior project. Again, the failure rate is very low, and students are not apprehensive or anxious about the examination.

At Santa Cruz every senior must pass a comprehensive administered by his board of study (department) or in some instances may be permitted to write a thesis instead. According to the registrar, approximately 10 percent of the students write a thesis each year. Each board sets its own policy. A student working under an interdisciplinary major receives an examination created by his advisors, while students with double majors generally take two examinations. The examinations are graded honors/pass/fail, and those who fail must repeat the examination. Two failures may keep a student from graduating. Examination formats vary by subject area. For example, students in the fine arts must assemble a one-man show, those in the sciences must engage in research activities, and those in literature must take a test based on a list of thirty to forty books.

Faculty and students both like the idea of the examination, although many students said that they were not given enough information to prepare adequately for it. Its major strength, in their opinion, is that it helps students synthesize what they have learned. Its major weakness is that it is administered with varying degrees of seriousness in different departments and that it gives rise to some anxiety. In addition, some students felt that the requirement is a burden and does not provide a sufficient reward.

Senior Projects

Senior projects were studied at Bard, Reed, and New College. Bard requires each student to complete a senior project, which accounts for one course each semester of the senior year. The nature of the project varies from division to division: from artistic project, to laboratory research, to translation of a foreign work, to critical paper. The topic for the senior project must in theory be approved by the divisional faculty, though, in fact, the job is lodged largely with the student's advisor. The analysis of the completed project by the division includes, as did the comprehensive, an oral examination before a faculty board.

The senior project is by far the most popular feature of the Bard curriculum. Over three fourths of the students and a large majority of the faculty expressed enthusiasm for the project. They approved particularly of the close contact between students and faculty, the opportunity provided for independent study, and the psychological benefits (feelings of self-confidence and competence) resulting from such a project. Students felt no anxiety toward the senior project, although 40 percent of the same Bard sample had expressed anxiety concerning the moderation previously discussed.

At New College one quarter of each student's last year is devoted to preparing a thesis. However, because students are already required to complete a certain number of independent studies, the senior project did not provide the same breath of fresh air it did at Bard. Students and faculty were pleased with it, but it was simply considered an extended independent-study project.

At Reed College the senior thesis received the same over-whelming enthusiasm as was noted at Bard. The program is struc-tured and administered similarly at the two schools, although the Reed administration seems to regard it as an even more central part of the curriculum. Many students and faculty consider the thesis the best part of the Reed curriculum. The members of the student sam-ple already working on their theses expressed unqualified enthu-siasm, while most other students were looking forward to beginning the thesis. The quality of work produced is apparently so high, and so often cited, that a small number of students expressed fear of being unequal to the task. Several theses each year are published in professional journals.

Senior Seminars

Senior seminars have proved unsuccessful at New College, only moderately successful at Justin Morrill, and quite successful at Bowdoin. The New College senior-seminar effort has already been abandoned. According to the college's plan, students were to devote the first and third years to diversified course work and the second to a major. One element of the third-year program was to be the senior seminars, which were to be interdisciplinary offerings. In 1968 the seminars were dropped because, according to a 1970 in-stitutional report, the seniors were already too specialized for inter-disciplinary work; and a "uniform and relevant" program could not be found. Similarly, a senior-seminar program at Justin Morrill College, structured as an interdisciplinary, team-taught course, has been remodeled, owing to student dissatisfaction and the excessive costs inherent in team teaching. The current seminar program, re-introduced in fall 1970, is a more modest undertaking with three or four sections per semester, each taught by individual faculty, for the two hundred seniors. As was pointed out in the discussion of freshman seminars, those classes with topics and structures pre-determined by the professors fared better than unstructured courses —a sad fact for those who expected seniors to develop independent learning abilities through four years of college.

Bowdoin College has made one of the most comprehensive attempts in the country to reexamine and rebuild the senior year. In 1964 Bowdoin established a senior center and a program of senior seminars. The seminars, with which professors are encouraged to experiment, have roughly the same general structure: a few weeks of class meetings at the start of the term; then a lengthy period in which each student works on a topic-related project, either individually or as part of a group; then further class meetings, where students discuss their work on the projects. Coordination of seminars is achieved through staff meetings held twice a semester. Seminars usually are limited to fifteen students and are graded on an honors/pass/fail basis.

All faculty are approached to teach in the program, and twenty to twenty-five seminars are mounted each year for the approximately two hundred seniors. The voluntary participation of instructors was felt by some faculty to enhance their motivation. Faculty must obtain departmental permission to participate in the seminar, since the course counts as part of their teaching load and is financed by their department. The director of the seminar program said that he has had good cooperation from the faculty and that professors from all departments have participated. From the start of the seminar program in 1964 through the spring of 1970, full professors, surprisingly, formed the largest contingent in the volunteer teaching staff; professors from the three divisions—humanities, social science, and natural science—have participated in relatively equal numbers. Students, on the other hand, have shown little initiative or creativity in responding when asked to suggest seminar topics.

When the program started, seniors were required to take one seminar each semester. In 1967 the requirement was reduced to one seminar during the year, and in 1970 the requirement was dropped. During the period from 1967 to 1970, when one seminar was required, approximately two thirds of the seniors took two seminars. In the first year following the elimination of any seminar requirement, 89 percent of the seniors took at least one seminar. Among the seminars offered in fall 1970 were Friedrich Nietzsche: A Problematic Figure of Our Time, Environmental Decision-Making: The Citizen's Role in Land Use Planning in Maine, and The Artist as Philosopher.

Students approved of the loose, informal nature of seminars and the opportunity for freedom and independent study; they complained of lack of participation by seminar members, the assumption by the instructor of too much student background, and a lack of academic content in the courses. They seldom rated the program on the objectives for which it was initiated. For example, only one student commented on the nonmajor emphasis of the seminar. On the other hand, faculty commented chiefly upon the philosophic basis of the program. Many of them were enthusiastic about this opportunity to teach motivated students outside their discipline. Some of them have used the seminars to test possible departmental course offerings. Thus, a 1966 senior seminar on Africa: The Politics of Development became a freshman course in 1967. More important, the faculty also use the seminars as a laboratory to experiment with new teaching methodologies, which many have brought back to their departmental classrooms.

Although most students said that they did less work in the seminar than in other courses, the seminars at least seem to have succeeded in combating concentration parochialism. That is, more than half of the students enrolled in seminars whose subject was outside their school.

One of the most admirable features of the senior program is its annual evaluation by a council composed of six faculty members and, now, four students. The evaluation reports have been candid and well prepared and healthily responsive to student and faculty opinion. Thus, for example, the duration of the three phases of the seminar, which had been quite uniform, now varies from course to course at the suggestion of an earlier report; and professors who taught successful seminars are now encouraged to repeat them, whereas the original idea had been to offer each seminar for only one year.

The Bowdoin seminar program is part of a comprehensive senior program housed in a senior center, a small complex of dormitories with facilities that house the senior class and a small number of faculty. The center contains a dining room, guest apartments, recreational rooms, and common rooms, and is used almost exclusively by the senior class. Activities taking place in the senior center include concerts, lectures, some classes, and many of the senior seminars. Isolating all members of the senior class into one dormitory complex evoked little reaction from any sample members.

The senior center has an annual budget of $35,000 to $40,000, which pays visiting lecturers, student employment, secretary salaries, and travel allotments. If the cost of the faculty time for seminars, which is absorbed by the departments, is included, the budget is close to $100,000, and even this figure ignores the maintenance of the center.

The director of the center indicated that senior seminars may not be as necessary as they were in 1964, since Bowdoin now has more small classes and more opportunities for independent study and since the freshman and sophomore distribution courses, which the seminars were intended to complement, no longer exist. Similarly, a majority of seniors felt that the seminars could be offered in any year.

The center has in any event made Bowdoin more receptive to innovation. Although the college was generally considered somewhat conservative academically before the program was started, Bowdoin has since made a number of changes which challenge that reputation. For example, it has loosened its grading system, it has created a number of interdisciplinary course offerings; and it now permits students to create their own majors. The mere presence of an innovation as imposing and grand as the senior center exerts itself strongly upon the life of the Bowdoin community, making the prospect of change less threatening and thus opening the community to additional change.

Conclusion

Comprehensive examinations appear to be less than a stunning success. While many professors at each of the colleges expressed justifiable enthusiasm for the idea of asking each student to review his progress, few students outside of Santa Cruz found this process to be a significant part of the comprehensive. The fact that the examinations are graded tends to make the experience a mere certification, stressing passage instead of information transfer and individual growth. In addition, the lack of rigor, manifest in the low failure rate, precludes deep review and study of the previous two, three, or four years. Nonetheless, at least a few students in each sample did derive some value from the examination, and it seemed harmful to only one or two. (For example, a student at Santa Cruz switched her major to avoid what she understood to be a particularly rigorous comprehensive.) The negative effects created by the examination can be mitigated if students are better informed of its nature and purpose. The harder question, however, is how to make the experience meaningful for more students.

An answer may be provided by the model of the Freshman Inquiry program initiated at Haverford in 1971 (see Chapter Two). This model would turn the examination, regardless of the year in which it is given, into an oral advisory session. Thus, sophomores or freshmen might discuss their plans for study and determine whether their intended major is really best suited to their needs; juniors or seniors could discuss what they have learned, what they want to do next, and how best to proceed. As this model recognizes, the use of comprehensives to weed out unqualified students has failed; and their use as plain examinations is unnecessary in a system that already has college boards, graded courses, and various types of standardized graduate examinations. If a satisfactory advising function for the structure created by comprehensives can be devised, it should be used. If not, the comprehensive should be abolished.

Of the three senior-seminar programs studied, only Bowdoin's has become an even remotely important part of the student's college experience. Bowdoin's relative success is attributable to the well-planned nature of the program; the active participation of students, faculty, and administrators; and the availability of funding commensurate with the needs of a comprehensive program. Nevertheless, even a well-administered senior-seminar program like Bowdoin's will noticeably alter the education of few students. For most, the seminar, even if it is good, is merely one course dwarfed in a year spent fulfilling concentration requirements and does little to topple the pyramid of narrowing specialization found in the college years. Expansion of the single course into an academically comprehensive senior program will be necessary to balance and place in perspective the emphasis upon concentration in the last two years of college. Any successful effort must involve the commitment of faculty, administrators, and students in a comprehensive program such as the senior thesis at Reed or the senior program at Bowdoin, which also required a substantial allocation of funds.

While the institution of the senior thesis was the most successful offering studied, examination of the other programs has been important if only for pointing to the barrenness of the senior year at most colleges. If colleges maintain the length of the student's tour of duty at four years, or even three or five years, the programs ultimately selected must reflect the changing needs of students in each academic year and the goals of the institution.

Concentration

𝕬𝕬𝕬𝕬𝕬𝕬𝕬𝕬𝕬𝕬𝕬𝕬𝕬𝕬𝕬𝕬𝕶𝕶𝕶𝕶𝕶𝕶𝕶𝕶𝕶𝕶𝕶𝕶𝕶𝕶𝕶

With the gradual dilution of general education, concentration has become the prime focus of the undergraduate college. As the process of dilution occurred, the first two years of college education lost their purpose. And when no substitute was offered, it was only natural that, by default, concentration filled the gap, since colleges are organized and faculty are trained according to specialty. But natural or not, the unfortunate result is that additional specialization has been substituted for a failing breadth program.

Admittedly, colleges have tried to lessen this emphasis on concentration. In the past most concentration programs absorbed about half of a student's course selections. Recently, however, departments in the social sciences, humanities, and arts have lessened their requirements, so that only one fourth to one third of a student's courses must be in his major, and have reduced the number of specific requirements to as few as one or two common courses; in fact, numerous departments do not specify any required upper-level courses. Departments in the natural sciences have, in most cases, maintained the large number of required courses, many of which are specifically designated. This, combined with a required sequential order, forces the science concentrator to commit himself to his major much earlier, generally at the start of the freshman year.

Trial Major

Concentration is connected directly to the manner in which the faculty is organized. Under the traditional division/discipline structure, each student must choose a discipline in which to concentrate. At schools like the University of Wisconsin at Green Bay, which organize their faculty through theme-oriented groups, the student similarly majors in one of the interdisciplinary organizations. Students are usually asked to select a tentative major at the start of the freshman year and to make a definite declaration by the end of the first year.

Bard formalizes this procedure by having a trial major during the freshman year. All freshmen must select a major and take two of their four courses in that field. A student may change majors as often as desired; however, several departments require a basic background obtainable through specified courses to be taken prior to a student's acceptance as a major in the sophomore year.

The trial major was intended to quickly expose students to both breadth and depth; but it has become, in the words of a Bard administrator, only "the fossilized remains of a program." And most of the students and faculty interviewed regard the trial major as useless, since students almost always go through a succession of alternate majors and discard the concentrated trial major. Some students even consider it detrimental because of the course-selection restriction it imposes—the requirement of two courses in one area and the practice by several departments of offering courses for trial majors alone. In addition, some faculty felt that students become trapped by their trial major. On the other hand, a very few students felt that the trial major had saved them from majoring in an area they would have disliked. Despite these remarks, the trial-major concept seems to provide only a needless formalization of a simple process employed without requirement by many colleges.

Double and Joint Majors

A few schools have tried to avoid the standard departmental majors completely (New College at Hofstra University in New York requires only that students concentrate in one of four divisions)'. Others have added options to complement the traditional system. The simplest of such offerings is the double major, studied at Haverford and Santa Cruz, which necessitates a student's completion of all the requirements of two departments. Because a double major requires a large percentage of a student's course load, few use the option. Whether or not this option is formally available at a college, it is theoretically possible for any student to have a double major by completing the requirements of any two departments. Haverford, however, regulates double majors by reserving their use for high-ranking students, who must obtain permission from the associate dean and from the chairman of each department concerned.

Students take double majors mainly because they are interested in two disparate fields or in a field covered by two departments such as social psychology, political economy, biochemistry. For the latter reason, some schools offer the possibility of a joint major. Santa Cruz's employment of this option is typical. A student must receive permission to construct a program fulfilling most of the course requirements of two departments. The comprehensive major examination, required at Santa Cruz, is satisfied for the joint major by the administration of an examination prepared by the participating departments. Haverford's double majors are similar, although the chairman of one of the departments serves as the student's advisor.

Double and joint majors are rarely undertaken (9 percent at Haverford and 7 percent at Santa Cruz), though they have in general been satisfactory for students employing the option. Participation has been low, and few schools formally offer such options, mainly because a student with interests extending beyond one department can usually major in a recognized field and still find time to take the courses he wants in another. In the natural sciences, where such flexibility is more difficult, most students do not even consider double and joint majors.

Interdepartmental Majors

The specified interdepartmental major is another alternative to traditional majors. It merely institutionalizes the ad hoc joint major. Reed offers such majors in american studies, international studies, history-literature, mathematics-economics, mathematics-sociology, philosophy-literature, philosophy-religion, and special programs temporarily linking different disciplines. In 1971 about 8 percent of the seniors graduated with interdepartmental majors. Yale offers a similar option, called Special Majors, which attracts fewer than fifty students a year. Majors are offered in history and the arts and letters, social science, culture and behavior, and combined sciences. Trinity offers three interdepartmental majors, and Brown offers fourteen. Such programs are developed as a result of student persistence, faculty interest, or a combination of the two. The major is approved as a "program" with the ability to offer courses and grant degrees but without a budget (except minimal operating expenses) or distinct faculty. It is almost an ironclad rule that faculty can be hired only by departments. No general rules for the operation of such programs were found.

Because these programs have no budget and must rely upon courtesy appointments, they are ill equipped to grow with increased enrollments or even fend for themselves in a departmental environment; as a result, the largest programs have been forced to seek departmental status in order to survive. Faculties, however, have been reticent to support such transformation for fear of departmental funding loss following affirmative action. At Brandeis the American Civilization program, which had attracted an unexpectedly large number of concentrators, in 1970 was raised from its status as an interdisciplinary program to a department by a very divided faculty after a battle of many years. However, since interdisciplinary programs rarely go the full route to becoming departments, the increase in number of university departments has not become flagrant.

Student-Created Majors

A more significant modification of the concentration system is the addition of student-created majors. This option, which allows students interested in nondepartmental areas to form their own programs, has been adopted by many schools in recent years. Nearly all the sample schools requiring traditional majors offer this option. Student-created majors were studied at Antioch, Bowdoin, Brown, Haverford, Reed, Stanford, Santa Cruz, Trinity, and Yale.

The student-created major is the easiest mechanism to establish in order to give students the widest latitude of choice in major study. Most of the student-created majors observed in the study either combine two or occasionally three disciplines or focus on a specific period, problem, or culture by using material from several departments. Japanese Studies, Urban Problems and Design, Nineteenth Century Intellectual History, and Computer Science Math and Philosophy are examples of student creations. While many such programs encompass material exclusively from one division, a significant number are interschool proposals. At Antioch, in fact, most of the student-created majors in 1968–1969 and 1969–1970 relied on material from more than one school. Because of the prerequisites and hierarchical nature of courses in most science departments, the natural sciences are least often part of such programs.

The structure of student-created concentrations is remarkably similar at each of the schools studied. No school reserves this option for a select group such as honors students. Rather, any student can write a proposal for a concentration—including, in most cases, a description of the courses and independent study he plans to undertake and, where relevant, a proposal for a senior project. The number of courses required for a student-created concentration is usually the same as that required for the average departmental major, and schools that require a senior project or examination (see Chapter Four) easily fit that institution into their student-created majors. At Reed, for example, the senior thesis for such students is administered and evaluated by a committee of representatives from each department involved in the student's program.

The procedure for approval of a student-created major usually involves consultation with a number of people—advisors, department chairmen, and prospective teachers—so that before a proposal is formally considered, it has been either discouraged or molded into a form corresponding to the guidelines of the university-wide committee administering such programs. As a result, few proposals considered by the committee are rejected or returned for student modification. At Yale, for example, sixty-four of sixty-eight student-created programs proposed in 1970–1971 were approved, including six initially returned for revision; at Trinity fifteen out of sixteen were approved. Faculty at several schools expressed a fear or skepticism of student proposals with mystical or politically radical orientations. Yet such programs were very rare at all of the nine schools.

The number of student-created majors has been small at each of the schools. Although officials at a number of schools reported that the interest in such programs has increased dramatically within the last two years, in 1971 and 1972 most of the schools studied had less than 6 percent of their students participating in majors of their own design; the only exception was Antioch, with 12 percent. Figures for nontraditional majors, however, can be enlarged by the inclusion of the number of proposals rejected, ultimately unsubmitted, and undertaken within other options such as double majors or prestructured interdisciplinary majors. At Brown, for example, a significant number of students concentrate in the fifteen formal interdepartmental programs available. At Haverford, in each year's class of approximately 160, ten to twelve students are in double majors, five or six are in interdisciplinary programs, and three or four create their own majors—a substantial figure of 12.5 percent involved in interdisciplinary programs. Still, one Haverford administrator said that there is "very little use of the flexibility available."

Although such expressions of disappointment were common among the administrators and faculty interviewed, a majority of the faculty sample had formed no opinion of student-created majors, having had no experience with the program. Nevertheless, those who had had experience with student-created majors were enthusiastic about the concept and satisfied with all or most of the programs. Professors at all schools praised the flexibility and opportunity provided for students, especially the more aggressive and self-directed. Most faculty considered the programs at least as coherent as departmental majors.

On the other hand, a few professors interviewed at each school believe that work in a discipline is necessary to provide a respectable education and an adequate preparation for graduate school. Students and faculty alike feared a negative graduate school reaction to student-created majors. However, so few have been completed that an accurate assessment is not possible. Other reservations were that some students create a special major only to avoid specific requirements and that some of the programs created could easily have been housed in one department. Several faculty, on the other hand, thought that the majors might exceed the resources and expertise available at the college (probably a rare phenomenon, although an oriental studies major was found at a school with no oriental studies facilities)'.

Student-created majors, indicating large student interest in a specific area, occasionally have been the impetus for institutionalization of interdisciplinary programs. At Antioch, for example, the demand has been so great for interdepartmental majors of international studies, environmental studies, prelaw, and social work that formal programs have been organized and additional professors hired.

In view of the positive experiences and reactions to student-created majors, it is difficult to understand why so few students have employed the option. A primary factor at several schools seemed to be a lack of awareness of the existence of the option. At most schools this ignorance was the fault of the students and their advisors; but at Bowdoin, Wesleyan, and the University of Wisconsin at Green Bay, administrators, including registrars and deans, were unaware of the existence of this option at their school despite the inclusion of a description in the catalog. Such descriptions alone are apparently insufficient to perpetuate a program. This maxim is well demonstrated by the history of student-created majors at Brown. In 1969, when the Brown curriculum was dramatically revised, student-initiated concentration was part of the package approved by the faculty. Since the late 1940s the Brown catalog had mentioned the student-created major as a permissible form of concentration, but the option was not used prior to the more-publicized curriculum change. Following the change, 4 percent of the students chose to construct their own majors—even though departmental requirements had been reduced, made less specific, or expanded to include other options in twelve departments; and subsequent growth has been noted despite continued departmental liberalization.

A small number of students said that they had abandoned their major proposal because of a lack of faculty encouragement.

Similarly, a report by the Yale dean of student's office warns of problems for the student with an interdepartmental major: "He is, in effect, in a program by himself [and] must forfeit some of the services normally provided as part of a departmental . . . major." He therefore must find his own advisors, acquire the necessary background and sustaining interest without much outside help, and often convince graduate schools and others of the inherent value of a program they have never previously been presented with.

The lack of interest and occasional hostility regarding student-created majors by administrators and faculty, together with the legitimate warnings publicized by schools like Yale, put strong pressure on the student to choose a departmental major. The associated lack of bureaucratic red tape increases the desirability of departmental majors for many students. In addition, many students fulfill their needs through standing departments; others, though not entirely happy with any one discipline, either lack sufficient direction to create their own major or find the requirements of one department sufficiently flexible to permit the addition of many electives—particularly since some departments, as at Brown, have loosened their requirements and/or offer formal interdisciplinary options. Yet the departments at Antioch, where many students design their own major, offer great latitude, with few specific courses required. The fact that high student involvement in such a program is found at a school with attractive departmental requirements might be attributed to Antioch's policy of seeking students "who are ready to assume responsibility for their own lives . . . and for their own learning" (1970–1971 catalog, p. 192), accordingly drawing a more independent and self-directed student body. This unique-student hypothesis is strengthened by a work-study program that requires students to work independently for half of their college years.

Student-created majors, then, seem to be an option of value to only a small percentage of the students at sample schools. There is no reason to suggest that the programs are failures because they cannot compete in numbers with traditional majors. However, if student-created majors are to have real standing at most institutions, a program similar to that of Justin Morrill seems necessary. Upon reaching the junior year all Justin Morrill students are expected to choose a faculty member to serve as a concentration advisor and assist the student in planning a major program. The concentration can be either departmental or interdepartmental; it may be anything that meets certain credit requirements and that the faculty member will approve. In recent years, 40 to 50 percent of the majors have been standard departmental concentrations, while others have closely resembled them.

Required student-created majors force each student to address the question of what he wants to learn in college, encourage the planning of programs rather than mere enrollment in random courses, and can be initiated without disturbing the prevalent disciplinary organization of the faculty. On the other hand, such a program in schools lacking Justin Morrill's enormous faculty-student contact time would not provide the student with sufficient guidance. In addition, a faculty review board designed to maintain academic quality, usually included in student-created major programs, would become very costly, requiring an enormous commitment of faculty time. The omission of such a board, however, enhances the possibility of all the potential problems attributed to student-created majors.

No Majors

Three schools not having concentration programs were studied. One of them, discussed at length in Chapter Two, is St. John's; the other two, Sarah Lawrence and New College, are more conventional in orientation.

Sarah Lawrence has no formal mechanism for concentration. In fact, it attempts to enforce breadth by requiring students to take each of their three courses each term in a different department. Juniors and seniors are permitted, with the perfunctory permission of a committee, to take a "two-thirds program," with two courses in the same field. In 1971, 48 percent of the seniors and 19 percent of the juniors opted for a two-thirds program. It is, however, possible to achieve the equivalent of a traditional major by taking a course each semester in one department. Although these figures were not available, faculty members interviewed estimated that between half and three quarters of the students graduated with a major; approximately two thirds of the students in the sample plan to graduate with a major.

All but one professor said that they approve of the no-major idea and do not believe that students interested in graduate school will be adversely affected. A significant number of students, however, indicated problems with not having a major. Over two thirds of the students planning to concentrate felt they would be at a disadvantage after graduation because of the absence of official majoring. Several students interested in psychology, theater, and English said they were going to another school for a year to take the programs they thought they needed for graduate school. While this problem, felt by one fifth of the students, is serious and should be investigated, a significant contributing factor to the situation may also be the limited faculty size and course offerings available at Sarah Lawrence, which necessarily cause gaps in the curriculum.

An even more novel approach to concentration and course selection is the contract system adopted at New College in 1969. The college abolished official majoring and substituted an option to work under a contract each term. The central idea of the contractual program is that a student will develop, in term-by-term consultation with two faculty sponsors of his choosing, a program of courses and tutorials which meets his particular needs. The two sponsors must be from different departments. New College students were given the choice of declaring a major; and of the seventy 1971 graduates, thirty-one had done so. Since some of these students were carried over from the old program, which required a qualifying examination in a major area, the college recorder felt that the number of students declaring a major will drop. In 1972 the contract was adopted as a requirement for all New College students (see Chapter Seven).

Despite the novelty of concentration at Sarah Lawrence and New College and some student and faculty fears, neither school has experienced any difficulty in having its students admitted to excellent graduate schools.

Conclusion

There is no reason to endorse one concentration scheme as optimal for all. The existence of schools with well-specified philosophies regarding concentration is important, but it is equally important that all faculty and student applicants be aware of the options available at such schools.

Since no concentration scheme was shown to have insurmountable structural difficulties or serious graduate school problems, the system that permits the greatest student latitude seems preferable as long as it does not conflict with established institutional philosophy and goals. That a major is not absolutely necessary to undergraduate education is indicated by three schools—Sarah Lawrence, St. John's, and New College—which are doing very well without them. However, if concentration is felt valuable and maintained, the initiation of student-created majors offers students the greatest degree of flexibility with the least associated costs for the school. Faculty, students, and administrators at schools utilizing student-created majors overwhelmingly felt their quality to be at least as high as that of departmental concentrations.

Initiation of required student-created majors would force students to think about and concretely plan their education, which a surprisingly large number of sample students, seniors as well as freshmen, had never done. Although this system has functioned excellently at Justin Morrill, a college with very high student-faculty contact time, implementation at larger schools would entail a much-increased outlay of time and money, though not necessarily prohibitive when contrasted with the impact upon students.

6

Alternatives to Departments

Since the 1890s most colleges and universities have departmentalized the knowledge they offer by dividing their faculty into administrative units based upon what have come to be known as disciplinary lines. The use of departments originally represented an efficient way to group faculties and the areas of knowledge they studied, and later to divide the money and facilities of the university, and still later to design and administer curriculum. The result of continually adding to the function of departments has been to make departments the only academic unit in the university. This, in turn, has led to the belief that departments are not just administrative conveniences but the naturally ordained divisions of knowledge. Sadly, scholars have accepted this loss of the fundamental unity of knowledge. In everyday life at the college, people are so separated by their departments that interaction between them has ceased; and nondisciplinary programs, notably in general education, have been eroded by specialization.

To counteract this force, some colleges have loosened or changed the organization of their faculty and/or departments. Other schools have created supplementary extradepartmental programs.

Extradepartmental programs and broader faculty organization, although initiated to combat the same difficulty, represent different means of attack. In utilizing a broader faculty organization, a college is striking at the root of the problem—trying to change faculty behavior by placing faculty in a new environment (for instance, an interdisciplinary organization) that makes the old behavior impossible. Extradepartmental programs do not fight the problem directly but begin with the assumption that change in faculty behavior is either not completely desirable or too difficult to accomplish. Instead, they seek to provide additional flexibility by creating an organized center for innovation on the campus.

Each method has its own special value. Broadening faculty organization is an appropriate method, for instance, for a school—preferably a new college—that wants to offer a distinctive program for which traditional faculty organization is unsuited. For an older school, with a partially tenured faculty and routinized faculty behavior patterns, extradepartmental programs would probably be more easily implemented. The extradepartmental program is also optimal for schools interested mainly in a quick way to give students more flexibility.

Alternative Faculty Structures

Several colleges, in order to counteract objections to traditional departmental structures, have tried to increase the importance of the larger academic divisions or schools—social science, science, and humanities. This approach was studied at Bard, Eckerd, New College, and Reed.

Bard considers divisions its major structural units, not only giving them the responsibility for faculty hiring but also requiring each student to apply to concentrate in a division. The Bard faculty indicated that the divisional structure has at times fostered greater interdepartmental contact but that little interdisciplinary work or

team teaching has resulted from this contact. Professors in departments with only one or two members felt most involved in the division; others acknowledged that as the school grew, the divisions
became unwieldy, forcing reliance on a smaller unit—the department.

Both Eckerd and New College started with an emphasis on
divisions, and the divisions have continued as the administrative unit
for faculty hiring and funding. At Eckerd, however, professors in
small departments find the division more important for course planning and meeting others than do faculty in larger departments. In
addition, professors in the natural sciences consider their department
a more significant unit than their division. Almost all faculty at New
College, on the other hand, approve of the functioning of their
divisions—probably because each professor at New College has almost complete freedom regarding what he teaches, so that he is less
subject to the constraints of an administrative unit. In addition, the
school is small enough that the resulting gaps in each department's
offerings are probably unavoidable. Despite the success of divisions,
however, there has been little team teaching at New College; and
the divisions have occasionally become as inner-directed as the
departments they seek to avoid.

Divisions at Reed serve as units responsible for administering
course offerings. Faculty hiring is conducted by search committees
composed of two professors from the appropriate department and
one from outside the division. Faculty reaction to the divisions was
consistent only within each division, indicating at least an accepted
relationship between each department and its division. Professors
in the history and social science division, for example, believe that
the division has precedence over its constituent departments, while
those in the division of mathematics and science consider their
division irrelevant. The division of literature and languages has
functioned well and makes most major decisions because, according
to those interviewed, the departments within it fit together logically.
There is no indication that the existence of divisions has encouraged
interdisciplinary work at Reed.

An emphasis on divisions, then, has limited beneficial effects
and eliminates few of the problems raised by departments. It does,
through the interaction necessitated by meetings, force professors to

meet colleagues outside their field, although, for at least these four schools, it did not produce the anticipated increase in interdisciplinary or team-taught courses. Divisions seem almost essential for schools with small faculties; as a result, divisions have been seriously suggested as decision-making units only in small schools. However, an inevitable chain of events follows the growth of a school employing a working divisional system. At Reed, for instance, the division of literature and languages has increased in size, so that a split into two divisions has been considered. If Reed continues to grow, perhaps the French professors will begin to dominate the languages division, and then will start to meet together to discuss their common and unique problems, and eventually will constitute a department, in fact if not in name.

Three other schools studied—the University of California at Santa Cruz, the University of Wisconsin at Green Bay (UWGB), and Prescott College—were each founded recently with interdisciplinary structures designed to avoid departmental domination.

Faculty hiring at Santa Cruz relies upon the university's cluster-college structure. Although the academic structure is divided into three standard divisions, the disciplinary units within each division, called boards of study, differ from departments in two ways: they have no budget, and they hire faculty only in conjunction with the Santa Cruz colleges. Thus, each professor must be connected with one college in addition to his board. The faculty offices, with the exception of those in the natural sciences, are grouped randomly within the colleges and not by department.

The faculty interviewed at Santa Cruz said that they are extremely satisfied with this arrangement because they can more easily get to know colleagues in other fields; moreover, departmental competition and jealousy are reduced, and interdisciplinary work is encouraged. The random assignment of faculty offices has also been responsible for some interdisciplinary efforts, since professors from varied fields often become friendly by virtue of these assignments. The faculty cited difficulties, however, in staff recruitment, since all appointments must be approved by both a college and a board, whose interests do not always coincide. Professors also noted that boards have little flexibility in making future plans and that there is occasional duplication of effort between the colleges and the boards.

More significantly, most of the professors in the natural sciences felt little attachment to the colleges, considering themselves members of a department constricted by lack of budget and the occasional necessity to compromise in hiring.

Despite the objections noted, the Santa Cruz structure seems to deal effectively with the problems raised by departmentalization in two of the three divisions; faculty in the third division feel unaffected but not harmed by the system. This structure may be especially effective at a school like Santa Cruz, where the faculty knew about the structure before they were hired and where, initially, little emphasis was placed on the graduate school. (As this emphasis has grown, faculty noted that the boards of study have grown in importance at the expense of the colleges.) However, even for other types of schools, the assignment of faculty offices on nondepartmental lines might be an easily implemented device for reducing departmental inbreeding and perhaps stimulating interdisciplinary team teaching.

Since its inception in 1966, Prescott has chosen to stray even further from the traditional departmental structure by offering a curriculum divided into five interdisciplinary teaching and research centers: the Center for Contemporary Civilization, the Center for Arts and Literature, the Center for Man and Environment, the Center for the Person, and the Center for Systems and Science. At each of Prescott's centers, courses are organized around a series of themes, which change from year to year. According to students and faculty interviewed, this arrangement has produced a directionless hodge-podge in the arts and literature center, which is by far the largest and most diverse of the centers. On the other hand, the next-largest center, Man and Environment, houses three apparently distinct departments—anthropology, biology, and geology—with anthropology described as "as much a department as any university undergraduate anthropology department, only more professional." The three other centers, each employing fewer than seven professors, have operated more effectively as interdisciplinary units; however, the Center for the Person is not an acceptable concentration area, and the small size of these three centers precludes internal departmental groupings.

Among the benefits of the center system, students and faculty cited the interdisciplinary contact, which has promoted interdisciplinary and team-taught projects. At the same time, a significant number of professors complained that the centers are growing more and more isolated and self-contained and that the level of interdisciplinary activity is not much higher than at more conventional schools. And many students complained that programs and offerings are either too diverse or too broad; a few said that they would have to go elsewhere to follow their interests. The student dissatisfaction stems more from the small size of Prescott and its continually changing curriculum than from the interdisciplinary centers. Some students, on the other hand, felt that the structure of the programs does permit them to pursue an area in depth.

A program similar in structure to Prescott's centers is being attempted at the University of Wisconsin's new campus in Green Bay. Unlike Prescott, UWGB focuses its entire curriculum on the environment; therefore, its centers and themes—called colleges and concentrations—are concerned with that issue. UWGB has four colleges, each sponsoring up to four concentrations: the College of Human Biology, the College of Environmental Sciences, the College of Community Sciences, and the College of Creative Communication. In addition, a School of Professional Studies attempts to fill the gaps left by the colleges by offering programs in teacher education, business and public administration, leisure sciences, mass communication, and social services.

Although the faculty is organized through the concentrations, it is also divided into "options." The options correspond to traditional disciplines, and students can select one to combine with their concentration. That is, the student first selects one of the eleven environmental theme concentrations offered and then can, if he wishes, choose one of the twenty-one options, which have faculty from several concentrations and colleges. In addition, he may take one of the preprofessional programs. The options are merely groupings of faculty; like the groupings at Santa Cruz, they have no budget, although they do help recruit and make recommendations for faculty hiring.

The faculty at UWGB had come to the college because they were attracted by its distinctive curricular structure. In their interviews, during the school's second year, they remained generally enthusiastic. However, they noted that some difficulty in faculty recruiting is being experienced by options and expressed fears that some areas have already become too departmentalized. Indeed, there is a very close correspondence between the themes of the colleges and traditional divisions at other schools. The College of Community Science is essentially a social science division, with 95 percent of its faculty affiliated with options in that area; the College of Creative Communication is a division of arts and humanities, with 97 percent of its faculty affiliated with options in those areas; and the Colleges of Environmental Sciences and Human Biology share the division of natural science, with all of their faculty from that area. However, it does reflect favorably upon the future of interdisciplinary work at UWGB that many of the concentrations suggest courses for their students in other concentrations and several options. It is also encouraging that each concentration includes at least two options, and most include four to six. Moreover, approximately 10 percent of the college's courses are team-taught.

None of the three colleges, however, have been completely successful in establishing an interdisciplinary structure. This is not to say that these programs have failed but that as long as departments are the most accepted form of academic organization at American colleges, an absence of leadership at the distinctive school will mean a return to the fold. Prescott, UWGB, and particularly Santa Cruz, because of its growing graduate school, will have to continually struggle—not against deliberate opposition but against the centripital force of inertia. For innovating institutions the critical period comes after the implementation in seeing the program through. Such programs are always on the verge of becoming and never achieve a true sense of stability.

Extradepartmental Programs

Extradepartmental programs take many different forms and are difficult to evaluate, since most are relatively new and, more important, are planned for very individual experiences. The chief obstacles afflicting these efforts are those noted for all the curricular structures examined; that is, faculty unwillingness to participate and student inability to use the mechanisms creatively. Nonetheless, student enrollment in the programs examined was generally high—so high that enrollment was not available for all interested students. In addition, increased faculty participation was obtained with the initiation of additional incentives.

University courses. Extradepartmental university-course programs were examined at Brown, Santa Cruz, and Trinity. All three programs include courses on pollution and film; courses, such as The Private or Commercial Pilot Certificate and Urban Design Studio, used to fill gaps in the curriculum; and interdisciplinary courses, such as Modes of Experience: Science, History, Philosophy, and the Arts.

Each year since 1969 faculty at Trinity have offered a number of interdisciplinary courses, called "college courses," outside the departmental structure. In 1970–1971 five such courses were given, decreasing by 1972–1973 to three. Any faculty member may teach one college course per year as a fourth course without departmental approval, or as a third course with departmental approval. Faculty indicated that most departments are unenthusiastic about the concept of college courses; and since no other tangible incentive is provided, it is not surprising that so few professors have volunteered. Opinion regarding the courses, from the small number of participants interviewed, varied markedly even within the same course. The faculty expressed little interest in or knowledge of the program, while several students noted that the courses are overcrowded.

Extradepartmental university courses at Brown have been equally disappointing. These existed well before a major curriculum change in 1969, but the curriculum committee responsible for the change proposed considerably expanding the number of offerings beyond the six existing at that time. Yet only fourteen such courses, taught by nine faculty, were offered in 1969–1970; the number decreased to ten, taught by eight instructors, in 1972–1973. Three each year were given by Brown's University Professor, the only member of the Brown faculty with no departmental affiliation. The courses are separate entities, not clearly connected parts of an integrated program; and formats vary from standard faculty lectures to student-structured and student-led seminars.

Although most faculty participants had found their experiences to be positive and indicated they had learned a great deal, their conceptions of what the program should be varied considerably, with several noting that they used the course as a laboratory to try new techniques and teaching styles. The only consistent complaint was that students demanded more structure, to the extent that one faculty member said he was forced to return to a "regular course format." The few students participating in these courses had extremely varied reactions. The only criticism lodged with any frequency was that so few university courses are offered that classes are overcrowded and many students excluded.

The lack of success of the university and college courses at Brown and Trinity should have been predictable, since these programs are virtually without support. The problems noted are inevitable for programs treated similarly. At both schools few faculty have participated in the program, and very few even indicated a desire to participate. The nonfunding of the programs serves to reinforce the faculty's lack of interest. Students regularly complained that too few courses are offered, so that they were turned away or forced into a large class. Furthermore, both programs consist of groups of entirely divergent courses, with no unity between them. Only the fact that departments do not offer such courses makes a university-course program necessary.

Conversely, the very existence of such a program at Santa Cruz would seem unnecessary, because the encouragement of interdisciplinary work has been a central concern of the planners of its curriculum and faculty structure. Nonetheless, several of the colleges at Santa Cruz have created structures to further facilitate interdisciplinary courses. Stevenson College, for example, offers college seminars which study specific cross-disciplinary topics in depth; and Crown, the college emphasizing the natural sciences, offers optional senior seminars with topics "often chosen to illustrate and to explore the interrelations between scientific and nonscientific disciplines."

Open-ended course programs. The extradepartmental open-ended course programs are courses prepared for individual students; groups of students; or groups composed of students, faculty, administrators, and community people. In each case these courses are chosen by an extradepartmental student-faculty committee from suggestions submitted by its constituency. Such programs were studied at Brandeis, Stanford, Tufts, and Yale. Brandeis offers the simplest program, providing only a handful of traditional courses;

Tufts has the largest program, going far beyond single-course formats in its offerings.

The program at Brandeis, called Flexible Curriculum, is administered by a student-faculty committee, though final approval of courses rests in the office of the dean of faculty, which has occasionally vetoed controversial ones. The program began in 1967 with four offerings and has since decreased in size because of lack of interest in the university community. The number of student and faculty suggestions for courses has been few—no more than ten in any term. Those courses offered, however, have been well attended, necessitating size limitations in several instances. The program has occasionally been used by students, in the words of a former dean of faculty, "to do their radical thing." One student group, for instance, tried to use the committee to pass a number of experimental-college courses that the regular curricular committee would not consider. Otherwise, according to most of those interviewed, the committee has functioned only routinely. The program has, however, been successful in having its courses picked up by departments. Four Flexible Curriculum courses were subsequently offered by departments—which is particularly significant, since only half of the participating instructors have been members of the regular Brandeis faculty. In 1972 Brandeis supplemented Flexible Curriculum with a university-course program offering a small number of courses.

Yale's program to sponsor nondepartmental courses is much larger than the program at Brandeis. Since 1968 the school has offered a program of residential-college seminars, given with full course credit and organized within each of Yale's twelve residential colleges. The seminars were established not only to provide an educational role for the colleges but also to provide a structure to accommodate course experimentation and immediate demands for presentation of specific material. Courses are limited to fifteen students, and most have enrollments between twelve and fifteen. Students from the sponsoring college are given preference, but all students are eligible for all seminars. By 1971 about 150 seminars were being offered and more than 200 proposed each year.

The seminars, suggested by students or faculty, must be approved by the Yale College Course Study Committee, the appropriate departments, the college's senior fellows committees, and perfunctorily the faculty. One committee member said that the committee often screens courses to ensure faculty approval and maintain the committee's good reputation. Most of the seminar leaders are from Yale, although many have infrequently taught undergraduates. Other teachers have included *New York Times* drama critic Vincent Canby, educator Jonathon Kozol, and playwright Arthur Miller.

Each residential college has a budget of approximately $22,000, from which departments are repaid $1500 to $2000 for each professor's time. Although departments are generally cooperative, the program's director said that some fight not to give up professors. He said, however, that there is a general acceptance and, in many cases, imitation of the seminars within departments.

The seminars—ranging in subjects from ecology, the philosophy of science, genetic manipulation, and university protest to broadcasting for social purposes—are all structured in the same manner. They meet for about three hours a week, either in one or two meetings, and most require a paper and/or a project. In many of them, each student must acquaint himself with a particular aspect of the topic and give an oral presentation to the class. Some of them combine field work with classroom activity; and in one seminar five professors from varied fields meet for lunch with ten students each week and discuss their current research and interests.

Both professors and students were overwhelmingly enthusiastic about their experiences with the residential-college seminars. Students, as reported in Yale's *Course Critique,* rated the seminars at the top of Yale's other departments. Professors cited especially the small classes, the informality and flexibility, the ability to get away from the department, and the intimate and friendly nature of the classes. They also appreciated the opportunity to present rarely offered subjects and to teach students outside their own departments, the lack of constraint on material, the lack of pressure, and the ease with which a new course can be brought into the curriculum. Finally, they praised the high level of student interest, the new opportunity provided to teach undergraduates, the excellent papers submitted, and the education offered the teacher. In short, most faculty thought teaching a residential-college seminar was fun. Students were impressed with the high level of discussion and the emphasis on individuality, freedom, and flexibility.

Weaknesses mentioned by professors were the different backgrounds of the students, the lack of real interest and effort on the part of some students, and the skeptical attitude of some departments. Also, several professors felt that "way-out, artsy-craftsy" courses do not work, and the dean noted that science courses for nonscience students have been generally unsuccessful. (The failure of such courses was a problem found in every program examined. More thinking obviously needs to go into this type of course.) Students were disappointed by the poor planning in some seminars, the many hurdles for course approval, and occasional variation in the students' and the professor's expectations for the course. For example, a seminar entitled Is a Just War Possible? turned out to be about the Peloponesian War.

Stanford has a more elaborate network of structures to initiate nondepartmental courses. Its oldest program, established in 1964, is Undergraduate Special Courses, which provides three types of offerings: traditional courses; experimental, interdisciplinary, and other innovative courses which professors find easier to offer outside their department; and student-initiated courses—courses suggested and often partly designed by students but usually taught by a professor. Students may take up to twelve Undergraduate Special Courses or thirty-six credits, whichever is less, during the four years. Courses offered in 1972–1973 included Europe as Seen Through Travel Literature, History of American Indian Education, Jewish Mysticism, Risk and Insurance, and Dance and Its Relationship to Society.

Participation for both students and faculty is voluntary and without departmental incentives and compensation. Nevertheless, the number of courses offered and the number of students enrolling have mushroomed. In five years the program grew from 14 courses with 208 students to 124 courses with 3503 participants. At the same time, the average class size has grown from 15 to 28.

A second nondepartmental program, the Stanford Workshops on Political and Social Issues (SWOPSI), was organized during the summer of 1969 in an attempt to turn the college curriculum "more directly toward urgent social and political problems." The program hopes to raise the political and social consciousness of the university, the residents of the surrounding communities, and the participants in each workshop.

SWOPSI presents primarily student-initiated, although not student-taught, courses. The courses are open to anyone, but only undergraduates receive course credit. In SWOPSI's first term ten courses—focusing mainly on issues that can be studied first hand—were offered on topics such as air pollution in the Bay Area, California logging policy, delivery of health services, university research policy, and disarmament negotiations. The program, while continuing to offer the same types of courses, has grown and appears to have leveled off at twenty to twenty-five courses a quarter.

Most of the workshops combine weekly seminar meetings with much independent research. Most are graded pass/fail, and each is provided with a small budget for expenses, although larger sums are available for workshops that wish, for example, to publish a report. Several of the workshops have released lengthy reports, which were credited with influencing specific local and state-wide policy decisions. By 1973 thirteen SWOPSI publications were available. The program has a budget of approximately $12,000 a year.

Stanford's third nondepartmental forum is the Student Center for Innovation in Research and Education (SCIRE), proposed by Stanford's student government and established for a one-year experiment in 1970–1971 (with a budget of $18,000). SCIRE is unique in that the impetus for any project must come from a student. The student must approach SCIRE's governing board (composed of six students and five professors) with a proposal for a project or course, and the board offers advice and decides whether and how much credit should be given (as many as twenty-seven credits can be allowed). If the board approves a proposal, the student must find a faculty advisor.

In SCIRE's first three quarters of operation, it received forty-seven proposals and approved thirty-four—twelve individual and twenty-two group projects which together enrolled 333 students. The individual projects included FM Station Research and Research in Environmental Law and Water Law; group projects included First-Year Bengali, Suicide, and Field Methods in Community Development. Of the thirteen projects turned down, six were immediately offered elsewhere and two were to be resubmitted. The method of grading is decided by each instructor; about half use letter grades, and half use pass/fail. The board found through a questionnaire that all students and faculty attracted to the program would participate again in SCIRE. Also, of the program's first fourteen offerings, seven appeared to be successful according to traditional course criteria, and two were just individual-directed studies; this total, while leaving a substantial number of failures, is a good average for an experimental program.

SCIRE's other function in its first year was to serve as a clearinghouse for information on any distinctive academic program or course at or near Stanford. In this capacity, SCIRE keeps a list of Stanford faculty members who would be interested in advising, either formally or informally, certain types of student-initiated programs. It also maintains a "paper bank," a system whereby alumni and other outside professionals volunteer to comment on student papers sent to them. This gives a student more feedback on a paper than just his professor's reaction.

Difficulties have arisen in SCIRE for which no solution has yet emerged. The major problem is the "disappointing" number of proposals received despite a publicity effort. In addition, few departments will allow students to use more than three of SCIRE's courses for formal concentration.

The most ambitious program studied to provide additional inputs to the curriculum is the Experimental College at Tufts. While this "college" has a wide range of offerings, it differs from the Residential College at the University of Michigan or Justin Morrill College at Michigan State University, for example, in that it cannot exempt a student from university requirements or substitute for a major. There are not, therefore, "Experimental College students" at Tufts; rather, all students may avail themselves of its offerings. The only limit imposed on individual Experimental College enrollment comes from the prevalent use of pass/fail in college courses, since three quarters of each student's courses must be letter graded for graduation. Some of these courses have even—upon individual petition—been accepted for major and distribution requirements.

The Experimental College, governed by a student-faculty board, started in 1964 by offering two seminars with combined enrollment of twenty-six. By 1970–1971 the board was turning down fifteen to twenty proposals per term to stick to a manageable, self-imposed limit. Through 1971 the size of the program had increased each year, reaching a peak of 105 seminars and 1566 enrollments. In both number of courses and enrollments, the college is now the fourth-largest department on campus.

Seminars are taught by faculty, undergraduate students, graduate students, and visitors to Tufts. Faculty, undergraduates, and visitors each constitute 30 percent of the teaching staff, with the remaining 10 percent coming from graduate ranks. All faculty who teach in the college also teach a regular course load, despite faculty legislation encouraging the contrary. The college is neither allowed to pay Tufts faculty nor financially able to reimburse their departments. Each course instructor is allowed only limited funds for course expenses. Undergraduates who teach in the Experimental College for the first time receive credit for two courses, since in addition to leading a course they take a seminar concerned with teaching. All student-led seminars must have a faculty sponsor, who is encouraged to attend classes and work with the seminar instructors in the teaching seminar. Faculty did not take this obligation seriously.

Class-size limits of twelve for freshmen and twenty for upperclassmen were imposed to encourage the student-teacher interaction lacking at Tufts, particularly in freshman courses. Because of the size limitations, students are excluded from many seminars, and the program coordinator estimated that twice as many students would be enrolled in these courses if there were room for them. Statistics compiled by the board of the college show that students compared their seminars very favorably with their other courses at Tufts. The only factor in which the seminars rated below other university courses was the amount of work put into each class. Students enrolled in seminars primarily because they were attracted by the subject of the course but also because they wanted a small, informal learning experience and the excitement of something "new" and "experimental" and, finally, because some college seminars are easier than other courses.

The student teachers almost universally found their experiences rewarding but, because the class was too diversified, not completely successful. They also complained that, because courses are pass/fail, students do not put maximum effort into them. Most also said that they would organize their material differently if they were to teach the course again.

The students taking courses taught by their peers rated them slightly below faculty-led courses in quality. Student objections usually had to do with the lack of coherence and structure of their seminar. They also said that they did less work for a student-led course. As early as 1968 the faculty evaluation of the college found student-led courses to be a source of concern for many faculty members. The evaluating committee recommended, however, only that the college board closely supervise such offerings.

Although visitors are not recruited for the Experimental College, a diversified group—including staff from the university, retired people from the surrounding area, and people active in various endeavors in the Boston area—have offered themselves each year. At least one of these people moved onto the regular university faculty after spending a year at the Experimental College. Visitors are the only teachers the college is authorized to pay, although efforts are being made to pay graduate students. The amount of payment is at the discretion of the board, and no visiting lecturer may be paid for more than two terms. The college often shares the cost of a visitor with a department; for example, the cost of a visitor offering a welfare-rights seminar was shared by the political science department, and the cost of a seminar on biology and education was split four ways. Again, students in courses taught by outsiders rated them below faculty-taught courses. Since a similar reaction was found for student-led courses, we can probably conclude that the problems in the courses arise from the teacher's lack of experience rather than from any special resentment of students toward undergraduates as teachers.

Although graduate students can teach in the college, few have done so—probably because they receive neither credit nor money for participation. Nevertheless, the board of the college hopes to attract more graduate students as some graduate departments give credit for teaching in the college and some money is made available for such service.

One aim of the Experimental College, and the seminar program specifically, is to move innovations into the university curriculum. It is for that reason that no teacher of a seminar can be paid more than twice, and few of the seminars have been offered more than twice. In recent years departments have been picking up two or three courses a year, or less than 5 percent of the college's offerings. Several of the language courses first offered in the college are well on their way to being incorporated in departmental offerings. Hebrew is now offered elsewhere in the university, and Japanese and Chinese are expected to follow shortly. Other Experimental College courses adopted by the university include courses in photography, film criticism, and dance; courses on women and blacks; and some political relations and history courses.

In addition to its seminar programs, the Experimental College has further distinguished itself by providing a number of other programs, including independent study and off-campus student teaching (see Chapter Seven). The college also sponsors Auditing for Breadth, Participant in Discovery, and a self-achievement program.

Auditing for Breadth allows a student to receive course credit for one course by auditing three over one or two semesters. This program, started in 1965, had attracted about two hundred students by the end of 1970–1971. Over fifty students had started and withdrawn. A study compiled by the program's designer in the spring of 1970 reported that the 151 students who had passed through the program had audited over 130 different courses in twenty-five departments. When the students were asked to rate their enthusiasm for the program as high, moderate, or low, 85 percent chose high. The most frequently cited strengths were the "broad exposure and removal of pressure"; the weakness mentioned most often was the difficulty in deciding which courses would be most beneficial to audit.

Participant in Discovery was started in 1969 to give students an opportunity to work with senior investigators on their research projects. The college sends a letter to all faculty members, including those in Tufts' medical and dental schools, asking whether they are doing research in which a student could participate. If a student expresses interest in one of the opportunities listed, an apprentice-like relationship, replacing one course in the students' program, is arranged for one semester. The Participant in Discovery option attracted forty to fifty students in each of its first two years and currently is able to offer a greater number of research opportunities than are demanded. To date, almost all offerings have been in the natural sciences.

The self-achievement program is intended for students who feel that they can better master the material of a course outside the classroom. Thus, students who have had difficulty with mathematics, for example, have used this option, rather than the course, to move more slowly and emphasize troublesome areas. A student in the self-achievement program works with a professor and must pass an examination. The program attracted only eight students in its first year, 1969–1970, but program officials believe that participation will increase.

Three programs in the Experimental College have already found a home elsewhere in the university. One is the Applied Physics Program, which was prevented entrance into the regular curriculum through a lack of agreement between the engineering and physics departments. A coordinated program which offered a student both a bachelor's and master's degree was originally placed in the college and then moved to the graduate school.

Finally, Introduction to Research and Scholarship is a program started by the Experimental College to help improve the writing of freshmen by matching each student with an upperclassman and a faculty advisor. The freshman and upperclassman meet together for three hours a week and with the advisor for one hour a week. Although the program is open to all freshmen, those with low verbal SAT scores are specifically invited into the program. An evaluation of this program conducted after its first semester of operation indicated that those who accepted invitation into the program achieved grades at the same level as the rest of the class, while those who declined received lower grades. In its first two years of operation, before it was adopted as a regular university program, the program attracted 137 freshmen out of a possible 600.

In short, the Experimental College, which started as a marginal effort, has grown to be a central part of the university curriculum. In six years enrollments have increased from less than 1 percent of the student body to a majority. The college clearly anticipated student desires, and students clearly made use of it. The college has also stimulated the introduction of new programs—programs that can be tested without implying a permanent commitment. In addition, through its involvement in the surrounding community, the college has positively affected the university's public image. Finally, the minor use of the college as a laboratory for experimentation with subject matter and teaching format necessarily influences faculty members when they return to their departmental classrooms. The 1970 evaluation of the college concludes, "The college, by providing an example of innovation, has improved the climate for change in the whole university."

On the other hand, there is a problem inherent in having a "center for change." That problem is that departments and individuals outside the center will abrogate all innovation to it and assume a position of greater stability and/or intransigence than they would have otherwise. Until recently, for example, some departments routinely sent most applications for independent study to the Experimental College. The college has also suffered from low faculty participation. In the words of the 1969–1970 chairman of the college board: "For several professors the Experimental College is one of the most exciting activities on the campus, where ideas and practice come together for once. Yet for most professors it is a waste of professional energies, since it is not a 'route to university or professional advancement.'" For example, the speaker himself was denied tenure and forced to leave Tufts.

The budget for the college's seventh year was approximately $28,000. The largest expense was salaries for visitors, which range up to $1000 each. Although this budget, by many standards, is small, its fourteenfold growth since the inception of the college may reflect the administration's enthusiasm. The 1970 evaluation viewed the college as a good investment:

In . . . cost of instruction, the Experimental College is a uniquely economical portion of the University. If a rough figure of 1600 en-

rollments in the college for 1969–1970 is divided into the budgeted $18,000, the cost per course enrollment comes to $11.25. . . . If students regard their tuition as the purchase of credits toward degrees . . . then each may be said now to spend roughly $2400 per year for thirty credits, or $80 a credit. Some 1600 student enrollments, typically at three credits a course or program, plus three additional credits for some seventy peer teachers this year, yields a total of over 5000 credits, representing the expenditure of some $400,000 in tuition. . . . It seems clear that, if there were no Experimental College at Tufts, the regular curriculum would be absorbing 1600 more course enrollments this year, in larger classes or in extra classes.

Conclusion

The emphasis on divisions at Bard, Eckerd, New College, and Reed, and the more ambitious attempts to improve upon the traditional departmental structure at Santa Cruz, University of Wisconsin at Green Bay, and Prescott point out the difficulties of successfully implementing structural change. Such innovations attack the problem of academic parochialism directly but require a constant struggle to be even minimally maintained.

On the other hand, open-ended extra departmental programs are successful in filling curriculum gaps at very low cost— much below that required for the establishment of a mushrooming number of ad hoc programs. For example, for $28,000, the cost of two faculty salaries, Tufts has offered 105 seminars and a plethora of additional programs. Such structures provide a degree of flexibility permitting rapid change, since all programs and courses are experimental and often have time limitations, so that initiation implies no long-term commitment. At most traditional universities with strong graduate and departmental orientations, such structures may be the only way to introduce a significant measure of flexibility within the curriculum. For achieving this goal, the small university-course programs at Brandeis, Brown, and Trinity are of minimal value; however, even such programs are not without merit, since they do provide courses in some lacking areas and maintain the understanding that knowledge does exist outside the departmental structure. Expansion of such programs makes good sense, since the negative effects noted were small.

The presence of the experimental programs at Stanford, Tufts, and Yale has encouraged some departments to avoid experimental undertakings and independent study; however, the innovative impact of the programs upon the university, through the adoption of innovations by the university and of courses by the departments, has been far more significant. It is regrettable, however, that these programs, created as alternatives to departments, still perpetuate the departmental vision by asking departments to approve their courses. Fortunately, departments are too lax to do this thoroughly. The open-ended extracurricular programs have succeeded in obtaining sufficient faculty to offer strong programs while also utilizing outside resource people, often from the immediate community. Student use of the innovative mechanisms within these programs has been low; however, student enrollment in courses has been high, so high that many have been turned away.

Movement of universities in this direction is an immediate short-term way to open curriculum, but at the same time it affirms the existence of departments and the narrow specialization that characterizes them. This situation probably cannot be remedied through the action of one university; rather, an alteration in the faculty reward system and professional-training programs will be necessary. In this sense, exposing undergraduates, who will be the future university faculties, to extradepartmental courses which offer greater latitude and different orientations of material studied is a good first long-term step.

7

Student-Centered Curriculum

Student-centered curriculum, which emphasizes educational planning by the student, is another departure from traditional departmental education. The student-centered approach makes the assumption that students are not identical passive containers to be filled with knowledge and discharged into the world but individuals capable of active and independent learning. The responsibility for students' education is thus placed squarely upon their own shoulders, and a growing self-reliance is encouraged. With this approach, classroom courses become only one way that a student can spend his time; and the notion of "requirements" no longer means simply how much time might be spent but what specifically occurs during that time. The professor also gains a new role. He or she becomes a resource person who not only can teach courses but also is available to give specific expert help and

96

advice. The addition of noncollege teachers, peer teachers, and self-teaching frees the faculty teacher, making him available for individual student contact. Most important, the student learns that education is not specific to the college and can be a lifelong process.

Today, much of the effort in student-centered curriculum is being spent on projects like University Without Walls (Union for Experimenting Colleges, Yellow Springs, Ohio), Empire State College (State University of New York, Saratoga, New York), and Campus-Free College (Arlington, Massachusetts), which use the world as their campus and are completely student oriented. Since the emphasis of this study was the campus-based college, we did not study external-degree and predominantly off-campus programs, however, we did examine independent-study programs of many varieties and peer-group teaching because they represent alternatives to classroom learning and traditional teaching.

Student Teaching

Student teaching of credit-bearing college courses was studied at six colleges: Antioch, Santa Cruz, Sarah Lawrence, Stanford, Tufts, and Trinity. (Student teaching at Stanford and Tufts is also discussed, as part of larger undertakings, in Chapter Six.) The programs are almost identical at each of the six schools. A course is initiated when an interested student writes a detailed course description, usually including a reading list and means of student and course evaluation. The student then selects a faculty advisor and submits the proposal to the appropriate committee for approval. Most of the courses are offered pass/fail, either through requirement or student option.

Santa Cruz alone has an explicit policy that only juniors and seniors can propose courses; yet this corresponds with the practice at the other schools. The courses usually have an upper limit for enrollment of between ten and twenty, and only Antioch requires a lower limit (five). At all schools the student teacher and other class participants receive credit for one course. Only at Tufts, as noted previously, is a seminar in teaching offered to the course initiators.

Few student-taught courses have been mounted at any of the schools. Santa Cruz offered eighteen in 1970–1971; Antioch and

Trinity have between five and ten a year; and Sarah Lawrence, which prominently displays the offering in its catalog, has only one or two annually. While one or two student proposals at each college have been turned down and the sizes of the schools differ, it is fair to conclude that only a very small percentage of the student body at any of the colleges has been attracted by the opportunity to teach a course. However, a significant number of students have enrolled in student-taught courses as participants. At Antioch, for example, which imposes no upper limit on class size, an average of 254 students enrolled in student-taught courses each term for the five terms from winter 1970 through winter 1971. Of this group 990 students took one course, 120 took two courses, 10 took three courses, and 2 students took four.

Student teachers universally found teaching to be difficult but worthwhile. While there was some disappointment expressed because of unanticipated problems and an inability to achieve all course goals, on balance every instructor interviewed was glad to have taught a course. Appraisals by the student participants and faculty sponsors were less positive. Most of the students were disappointed in the student-led courses and considered them worse than a faculty-led course. Nevertheless, enthusiasm did exist both for specific courses and for the concept of peer teaching. Some faculty sponsors and student participants praised the quality of the material, the flexibility and informality and occasional livliness of the class, and the obvious enthusiasm of the teacher; but most respondents complained of poor structure and the teacher's lack of classroom leadership and lack of knowledge—although the faculty were generally more charitable than the students, recognizing that the courses are "more exploratory than a professor's" and "a joint effort of all in the room." Several students who had not participated found the idea of enrolling in a peer-taught course inconceivable. A student at Sarah Lawrence said, "I can't understand why anyone would want to take [a student-taught course] when she could take a real course instead."

Even the best-run program of student-taught courses probably are more beneficial to the student teachers than to the student participants. Additional programs offered by Tufts and Trinity are therefore of great interest, since they permit undergraduates to design and teach courses for students in the public schools. These programs must be distinguished from the teacher-training programs that assign a student to an elementary or secondary school teacher and usually require full-time participation for one or two terms.)

Tufts, through its Experimental College, sponsors two programs that offer undergraduates a chance to teach and also are of assistance to the neighboring community. In one program Tufts arranged with the nearby city of Somerville to supply teachers—students, faculty, administrators, and friends of the university, the municipal government provides students, a building, and advertising. Although only a few courses have been offered, they have attracted a mixture of high school students and working men and women. In the other Tufts program six undergraduates and one administrator taught a course in English offered to the university's twenty-one Portuguese-speaking employees. The undergraduates received credit for one course, and their "students" received time off from work.

Trinity's high school seminar program offers undergraduates credit for teaching one course to high school students, who pay two dollars to enroll and do not receive credit for the course. The program has the approval of the local Secondary School Principals Association because it believes that the program "stimulates the intellectual interests of local high school students." Each Trinity student must have his course approved by a committee and supervised by a professor. At the end of the course, he is given a pass/fail evaluation by the professor. Between 15 and 20 percent of the course proposals have been rejected. Nineteen high school seminars were given in 1969–1970 and a greater number the following year. Courses have included Violence and Nonviolence, Sculpture in the Twentieth Century, and The Rise of Fascism—Germany: 1918–1933. This program has provided an extremely successful, and perhaps ideal, method for giving teaching experience to undergraduates. One student teacher said that participation in the program is probably the most educational experience at the college. While a few student-taught courses for other undergraduates can and should be offered, a program such as Trinity's can safely provide an opportunity for many more courses, since the effects of failure and student prejudices against it are smaller. The instructor will still gain even if the seminar does not succeed; and the high school students can benefit from the reading, consideration of the material, and interaction with course members.

Independent Study

Independent-study programs at undergraduate colleges have grown enormously in the last two decades. First offered only for honors students, they have come to be accepted for all students at many schools. Colleges generally have two goals in offering an independent-study program. First, they hope to encourage students to investigate an area of interest in their major. For this reason, the most prevalent structure is to allow upperclassmen to apply to the department in which they are majoring. Columbia University, for example, permits only seniors in certain departments to undertake an independent study. The second goal is a desire to expand the curriculum. While this is generally a less significant motivation, it is important at small schools with more limited curricula, since students are provided a range of topics few schools could afford to offer.

Many schools do little to encourage the use of their independent-study program. The feeling apparently is that such structures exist merely to accommodate the few students who are sufficiently motivated to seek them out. Some schools, however, actively encourage and seek to expand the use of independent study. Such programs were examined at Brown, Eckerd, Justin Morrill, New College, Santa Cruz, Trinity, Tufts, and Yale.

Santa Cruz often encourages students to substitute independent study for course work. In this case, the encouragement comes primarily from a faculty and administration who believe that such work is important rather than from any unique structure. As the catalog states, "Independent study is regarded no less seriously than the regular offerings of the faculty." There is no limit to the number of independent studies a student can take; and, upon permission, such studies can be counted toward concentration fulfillment. Each is taken with the sponsorship of a professor. Although all students are eligible to participate, independent study is intended for and used primarily by upperclassmen. About eight hundred independent studies are taken each quarter by Santa Cruz's 3000 students.

Santa Cruz, like other schools, often has more than one student investigating the same topic. While this is to be expected, it can cause a logistical problem; that is, one professor may be overburdened by sponsoring too many independent studies, or a number of different students may ask several different professors to sponsor the same independent-study topic. Brown has attempted to ameliorate this problem by instituting Group Independent Study Projects (GISP)'. GISPs are cooperative inquiries in which students have the major responsibility for planning and conducting the course work. These credited courses are each sponsored by an instructor, whose function is to approve the area and plan of the study, serve as course advisor, and evaluate the work of the course members. Graduate assistants, with departmental permission, can also sponsor GISPs. The proposals are reviewed by two committees to assure academic quality and avoid undue duplication. They are generally initiated by one or two students; others are then invited to sign up, and organizational meetings are held to begin the work. This program has been particularly popular in the social sciences and humanities. In 1968–1969, its first year, nineteen GISPs were developed, with enrollments of two hundred; the following year there were seventy-five projects and 685 students.

At Tufts departments allow students to undertake an independent study; and the Experimental College also has sponsored more than two hundred independent-study projects. These were projects that would not fit in a department because the student sought credit for more than one course or because the subject matter was not available in a department. All independent-study proposals have a faculty sponsor and are reviewed by a student-faculty committee. In addition, the college sponsors independent-study projects of one or two semesters, called Student Sabbaticals. The first one, sponsored in 1967, permitted a student to spend a semester in Spain combining a study of Spanish history and culture, an analysis of student political attitudes in Spain, and a photography project. In the first three years of the offering, there were six Student Sabbaticals.

At Justin Morrill and New College, students are not just permitted but required to pursue some independent study. New College requires students to complete four independent-study projects before they begin their final year. Such projects normally require prior approval of the student's advisor and one month of intensive work. Until formal concentration requirements were abandoned, at least one independent-study project had to concern a topic outside the division of the student's major. According to the independent-study coordinator, students are generally satisfied with their projects, but the faculty have sometimes complained that too little work is done on the projects. The faculty apparently are less pleased with off-campus independent-study projects (about 25 percent rated these projects only "fair-unsatisfactory") than with on-campus projects, presumably because they are able to regulate on-campus projects while in progress. It is surprising to find such difficulties in an offering introduced to increase the amount of freedom available to students.

Justin Morrill also requires some independent study, but in a form different from that at New College. Students are currently required to take twelve credits (three courses) of self-directed work through one project which consumes an entire quarter. It is preferred that such projects be undertaken off campus, but on-campus projects are permissible. Because independent study at Justin Morrill is designed to be a full quarter's activity, rather than an occasional substitute for courses, it can be planned more coherently than at New College. Each student takes a preparation seminar the term preceding his independent study, which includes journal maintenance and field-study experience. When the full-term independent study is undertaken, little counseling is available to the student. He is made aware of projects undertaken by others and of cooperating agencies and organizations known to the university, but he must make his own arrangements. Projects initiated by students have varied from sailing in the Mediterranean to learning a language at the Putney Institute in Vermont or living with a foreign family. The college contributes two thirds of the tuition for certain programs, and students are not permitted to earn money while on independent study in order to discourage students' simply working only in menial capacities to earn money, as they do in some work-study programs.

After the student returns from the independent study, he must take a follow-up seminar in which students report on their experiences and are helped to assimilate what they have learned. The entire independent-study experience, including both seminars, is graded pass/fail.

Although occasional poor placement seems to be the program's most serious problem, it is disappointing that an innovative and potentially exciting program such as this has failed to elicit great enthusiasm from the students. Many students were putting off the program as long as possible because no project or subject had captured their interest. Nevertheless, the program's director felt that it provides a valuable experience; and students returning from field study were often very enthusiastic about their experience, although it rarely led to further study.

If undergraduate college education is supposed to prepare students to study independently in the future, then a somewhat controlled initiation to such study undoubtedly should be an integral part of a college program. However, a program that merely pushes students out of the university for the sake of providing any independent experience will not produce meaningful experiences. Effective programs must rely upon a strong counseling system and have succeeded most fully when planned by students in areas of their specific interest. Initiation of the program described is more expensive, since it requires a counselor and placement staff. Furthermore, unless field experiences include salaried activities, experiences such as foreign study will result in added cost to the student or the university.

A more extensive independent-study program is the Scholars of the House program at Yale, created in the 1950s to allow a small number of students to design and pursue two full terms of independent work in the senior year. Students interested in this program meet with the appropriate committee chairman and then submit a letter of application containing a detailed description of the plan of work they propose to pursue. A faculty committee then interviews and selects the program's participants. The accepted students work with a faculty advisor, usually of their own choice, and are freed from formal course requirements. The Scholars of the House meet with the supervising committee every three weeks for dinner and a discussion of progress made by each student. Students also must present a progress report in December and, by May of the senior year, a finished essay or project "which must justify by its scope and quality the freedom which has been granted"; in addition, an oral examination, designed specifically for each student, must be passed.

To be eligible for the program, a student must have completed all distribution requirements by the end of the junior year. Students are not required to finish their department's concentration requirements, though prospective students for the program are urged to work intensively in their major during the junior year. Each year about 10 percent of the senior class (one hundred students) applies for the program, and ten to fifteen students are selected. In 1970–1971 the twelve students chosen studied such topics as field ion microscopy, the life and works of George Farquhar, and sixteenth-century architecture in Peru. The small number of students and the individual nature of their projects isolate the scholars and create a sense of loneliness, which is now partly alleviated by the addition of a triweekly meeting.

The Scholars of the House is an excellent program for those accepted. According to many of the people interviewed, the program is successful at least partly because the best students are selected or the participants are made to feel that they are the best students. It does seem unfortunate, however, that no effort is made to accommodate the approximately 9 percent of the senior class that is rejected each year.

At Trinity a relatively new program, called the Open Semester, provides a similar opportunity for students to pursue an uninterrupted independent study for one semester—preferably during the junior or senior year. The semester may be used to fill concentration requirements at the discretion of the appropriate department, but no provision is made to exempt students from any requirements. A professor serves as the semester advisor and is responsible for evaluating the Open Semester upon criteria established with the student. The semester is graded pass/fail. Unlike Yale's program, the Open Semester program is not limited in size. Nevertheless, only thirty-seven students enrolled the first year and seventy the second. Considering that the program was available to approximately one thousand students in those two years, the extent of interest shown was similar to that at Yale, although participation has been higher.

The program works with the Office of Educational Services in attempting to find appropriate Open Semester opportunities to match student interests. Topics have included Readings and Research in Epistemology, Researcher in a Gubernatorial Campaign, Cross-Cultural Coordination in the Peace Corps, and A Study of Hemingway.

The Open Semester program was considered a success for its participants. The program director rated the experiences of the first-year students as 38 percent "good-to-excellent," 46 percent "passable-to-good," and 16 percent "below par"; and the faculty advisors felt that the students had accomplished a great deal. A majority of the advisors interviewed further praised the program for providing an alternative for students who were tired of courses or Trinity and needed a break. The most prominent problems noted were a lack of student-advisor consultation, a lack of commitment on the part of some sponsoring agencies, and the substitution by some students of a whirlwind of activity for purposeful involvement.

The Jefferson House study program at Eckerd exempts participants from formal graduation requirements and allows them to design up to four years of study, in cooperation with one or more of the Eckerd professors associated with the program. Jefferson House is not a physical setting, and there is no commonality of living within the program. This lack of commonality was built into the program to avoid a situation smacking of elitism. The program consists of ninety students (8 percent of the student body) and nine faculty advisors. To be admitted, a student must explain to a faculty board what use he plans to make of the program. Admission has grown increasingly difficult, at least in part because some students have sought to enter Jefferson House to avoid Eckerd's core requirements (see Chapter Two).

The programs chosen by students in Jefferson House have been surprisingly traditional. According to several participating faculty, and confirmed by the students, over 80 percent of the students have chosen standard departmental majors and tended to specialize more intensely than students in the regular program. One student observed that the program is for "very directed and very undirected people." The emphasis to date has clearly been with the former group. One of the major strengths of the program appears to be the student-faculty contact established. Yet if the students are using Jefferson House to do little that they could not do without it, the program is probably taking faculty time and other resources from the rest of the college without great benefit to anyone.

Massachusetts Institute of Technology (MIT), in its Unified Science Study Program (USSP), offers an independent-study program for the freshman and sophomore years. During the summer of 1969 all MIT freshmen were sent a description of USSP as envisioned by the staff, with an invitation to probe further. One hundred of the freshmen (less than 10 percent of the freshman class) requested additional information, approximately forty-five spoke with the program staff during orientation week, and twenty-eight MIT students and several students from nearby community colleges subsequently enrolled. Students in the program are required to write a proposal describing the program intended and to pursue this program on their own initiative with the aid of the faculty core available. Students participate in USSP seminars (on such subjects as desalinization, James Joyce, and theoretical model making), individual USSP projects (on such subjects as housing in Guatemala and the study of mollusk and crustacean lipids), regular MIT courses, film series, and educational colloquia. Students in the program are also required to complete general MIT requirements. Program faculty consist of a dozen full-time-equivalent staff members, about a half-dozen teaching assistants, and approximately ten additional staff members available on an occasional basis. As a result of the large staff and small student enrollment, the program exceeds the regular cost per freshman at MIT. The first year of the program cost approximately $3000 per student. This cost is exceptionally high since it includes only costs related specifically to USSP. Of the forty-nine students who enrolled in the program during their freshman and sophomore years, only fifteen remained in spring 1971 at the termination of the first cycle. An equal number of program participants had left MIT entirely.

Many of the problems, strengths, and weaknesses in the program are discussed by Morgan (1970) and Schwartz (1970). Lack of definition was a problem noted by faculty and students.

Students also were disappointed with the advising, which was not connected with their academic work and did not provide sufficient feedback; and the faculty agreed that advising was weak. The failure of advising is a significant problem, since USSP is entirely dependent on self-evaluations. (Grading is strictly pass/fail.) In addition, students were unaware that their USSP work did not meet any of the general MIT requirements. As a result, after leaving the program students were made to compensate for their USSP freedom with a burden of heavy requirements, few electives, and the need to choose a major. With the institution of experimental programs, university requirements must be adjusted to permit the greatest opportunities for the success of these programs. Even more importantly, students must be informed explicitly of the position of the program relative to the rest of the university and the consequences of that position.

Comparing USSP with the regular program, students praised the regular program for its "expert guidance in selection and condensation of materials" and "the availability of faculty and resources." Some also liked the aspect of not having to cope with self-evaluation. Students complained however that the regular MIT program applied constant pressure while failing to give them time to think (Morgan, 1970).

New College has an orientation similar to that of Jefferson House and USSP, offering a contract system for all students for their entire college program. The contract (discussed briefly in Chapter Five) is a term-by-term plan developed by each student. It requires faculty sponsorship and can include any number of regular college courses, on-campus and off-campus experiences, and group or individual projects. According to an institutional self-study in 1970, 23 percent of the contractual programs were mostly individual projects and research, 44 percent were mostly regularly scheduled seminars, and 33 percent were combinations of seminars and individual work. The contract system, originally introduced as an option primarily for upperclassmen, attracted less than one quarter of them before it became a requirement in 1971–1972. Faculty involvement with contracts ranged from no sponsorships to four or five a year. All seemed to feel a desire to actively advise the contractors, but some acknowledged that this had been impossible because much of the work the students had done was off campus.

Others nevertheless demanded a weekly meeting or some form of written communication. Several said that they did not simply rubber-stamp contracts but often asked students to revise their proposals and even rejected some. Examples of contracts from the students interviewed include work on a campaign in New York, a study of draft evaders in Canada, and a paper written off-campus on fantasy literature. On-campus contracts relating to history, chemistry, and literature were also described. In 1970–1971 contracts were undertaken by a group of students who, as part of their contracts, agreed to live in one college residence hall and interact with each other.

Most faculty and students agreed with the philosophy of offering contracts, but some faculty were disappointed with the quality of work they had witnessed. However, faculty sponsoring contracts felt they provided a welcome opportunity to get close to students. Some faculty said a contract could be executed with virtually no faculty supervision and that sloppy work often resulted. A few also said that New College needs greater specialization than the contract system allows. One of the advantages of the contract system, however, is that it allows a student to make use of facilities not present at New College. Thus, one student interviewed was able to obtain an anthropology major although New College has no anthropology faculty. Another advantage is that students under contract get much individual faculty attention.

Conclusion

Peer-group teaching is the weakest student-centered program that we examined in our study. Since students have been taught to regard knowledge as something dispensed exclusively by an omniscient teacher, and consequently regard peer learning as inferior to teacher learning, most peer-taught courses could not be expected to succeed. The inbuilt lack of success does not imply, however, that courses taught by students should be eliminated; rather, they need to be seen for what they are—peer-group cooperative-learning efforts, as employed at Brown in the Group Independent Study Projects. This method groups together students with common learning interests, maximizes the learning feedback, and cuts down the number of individual independent studies. The GISP minimizes university costs through the use of faculty as resource people only; and it helps students begin to realize that other learning models—specifically, peer-group interaction—can provide excellent learning opportunities. For the students who merely want an opportunity to teach, the Trinity high school seminars and the Tufts community seminars would seem a better channeling of their efforts. Both programs are cost-free and provide community outreach, which is desirable for the community as well as university public relations.

The expansion of student-centered curriculum to independent study is a needed curricular development. Throughout this study we have found that students seem to be passively floating through their formal education, either unwilling or unable to think about what they want in that education. A required contract program, like that at New College, will force students, probably for the first time in many of their lives, to explore where they are going; and such exploration might shake them from their lethargy. For the off-campus segment of this program to work successfully, the student must be placed in an area that he chooses and that is related to his own interests. That is, unlike the Justin Morrill and Trinity programs described, the program must begin with the student and not with the available independent-study opportunities. Creation of an effective program of this nature will require a strong counseling and placement service, which implies additional costs. However, such costs might possibly be offset by decreased course enrollments.

Grading

Much of the reform in higher
education is aimed at providing students with a personalized education, as evidenced by the plethora of devices now available for concentration and offered as alternatives to departments. In grading, this
trend has caused a reaction against traditional letter grades, often
fostering efforts either to play down their importance by the use of
pass/fail or to provide more information for each student by use of
written evaluations. According to a 1972 study by the American
Association of Collegiate Registrars and Admissions Officers, 61
percent of all colleges have recently made grading changes, although
most of these changes involve only limited use of pass/fail. At the
same time, the growth of higher education, at least in absolute
numbers, makes it necessary to simplify transfer and graduate admissions techniques; as a result, admissions offices are now demanding straightforward letter and numerical grades. Thus, internal and
external university policies are at loggerheads.

The conflict causes an unsurprising bind for college students

and faculty. Many in the academic community have long characterized grades as mechanical and dehumanizing; as a result, both
students and faculty feel obliged to discount their value. At the same
time, they are well aware of the great impact of grades on students'
lives. Thus, although many of our interviewees claimed indifference
or neutrality toward grading—and even occasionally scoffed at interviewers for their interest in the subject—they talked longer about
grading than about other topics combined.

Grading systems were examined at twenty of the twenty-six
sample colleges; their experiences are the basis for the discussion of
grading structures.

Numerical and Letter Grades

Letter grades were studied at Reed and Trinity and numeri-
cal grades at Haverford. This material is supplemented by institu-
tional analyses on letter grades by Jacob Cohen at Brandeis
University and by the Committee on Academic Standards and
Procedures at Wesleyan University, and on numerical grades by the
Yale Daily at Yale University.

Student opinion regarding letter and numerical grades was
largely neutral to negative. Generally, students favored the abolition
of such grades and the implementation of pass/fail grading. Faculty
opinion, in contrast, ranged from slightly positive to slightly negative, with most neutral. The prevailing attitude seemed to be "All
grading systems are poor, but at least I'm used to this one and it's
easy to use."

The most frequent criticism by faculty and students of
numerical grades was overspecificity—presence of an excessive number of categories. Faculty indicated many methods for employing
the numerical system. Some use each number divisible by five or by
ten as reference points; others use an entire hundred-point scale.
Several use blanket grading (giving the same grade to all). Others
use various "point" systems; for example, one faculty member, using
a three-point system, gives 90 as his honors grade, 85 as passing,
and below 60 as failing.

The same situation prevails in letter-graded systems. The
Wesleyan study notes, "The faculty as a group has not enunciated
definitions of what various grades are supposed to mean, nor has it

any policy which defines its expectations about how the range of grades should fall. . . . We do not seem to know what particular notation should be used in order to indicate that a student is doing 'acceptable work.' " Similarly, a study of grading distributions at Trinity indicates wide discrepancies in departmental practices. For example, in one department 50 percent of the students received A grades; in another, only 11 percent received A's; in the college as a whole, 23 percent of the grades were A's. A similar variation was found for the other letter grades.

In addition to departmental discrepancies, at many schools grades in general are getting higher and higher. Studies of Brandeis, Trinity, Wesleyan, and Yale indicate excessive percentages of grades in the A and B range. A Yale collation of grades from 1963 to 1967, when numerical grades were abolished, shows a steadily increasing percentage of grades above 80 (from 59 percent in fall 1963 to 71 percent in spring 1967). At Brandeis the mean grade-point average for undergraduates rose from 2.81 in 1964–1965 to 3.17 in 1969–1970. At Trinity, in fall 1970, less than 20 percent of the grades were C, D, or F. At Wesleyan, in spring 1969 and fall 1970, 79 percent of the grades were A or B.

Reed has managed to avoid the inflation problem by establishing guidelines for grading distributions. The freshman grades are expected to be 15 percent A, 35 percent B, 40 percent C, and 10 percent D; for the sophomore through senior years they are 15 percent A, 45 percent B, 35 percent C, and 5 percent D. The distributions, according to the registrar, are followed except that there are fewer A's and D's than recommended. Faculty and students were basically neutral regarding the guidelines, though several faculty said that the rules are difficult to adjust to. As a result of the significantly lower grades, Reed students sometimes have difficulties with graduate and professional school admissions. That a school with Reed's reputation is having problems in this area shows how widespread the inflation of grades nationwide has become.

In view of the grade inflations, the grade-point average seems useless except for making gross discriminations. Our study does not substantiate the objectivity usually attributed to letter and numerical grades. Furthermore, professors, perhaps hoping to help their students by giving high grades, merely force graduate schools and employers to rely heavily upon the results of standardized tests, personal impressions, and influence. In addition, any feedback value the grade might have had for the student is negated.

But even worse, faculty give grades automatically and without thought. For instance, one of the studies notes: "(1) In several instances last semester, grades were turned in for students who had been absent from courses for the better part of the semester or who had left the university. (2) In at least one instance—and possibly more—students could be absent from [the college town] for significant blocks of time—up to six weeks and in one case about six months—and still receive credit for courses."

Written Evaluations

Written evaluations were examined at ten schools: Antioch, Bard, Brown, Eckerd, Haverford, the Residential College at the University of Michigan, New College, the University of California at Santa Cruz, Sarah Lawrence, and Wesleyan. Evaluations varying from a two-page single-spaced typewritten analysis of student performance to a single letter or sentence comment such as "A," "would give B— or 82," "a fine line separated the student and I and one day we crossed it" were observed. Most frequent were the single-sentence comments.

Evaluations, if they are taken at all seriously by faculty, are difficult and much more time consuming than grades. The grader does not have to rationalize his feelings as clearly in letter grades as he does in evaluations. The "good" evaluation minimally requires the author to review the student's entire performance and to enumerate the student's strengths and weaknesses. It involves more than merely writing the thought behind the previous letter grade; it requires, as most faculty indicated, an entirely new and different process. Nevertheless, the inability of professors to write evaluations highlights the barren and arbitrary nature of the letter grades they give without complaint.

Politeness is one of the shortcomings of written evaluations. Evaluators said that they are unable to tell the C student, "You lack ability and are wasting time in area Z." For this reason, several faculty admitted that they prefer the detachment and impersonality of letter grades. Giving a C says nothing about the student as a person. An occasional student agreed, feeling that his evaluations were too personal. A study at Haverford College, conducted by Associate Dean David Potter, indicated that Haverford professors consistently toned down evaluations—to the point of making them noninformational—for fear of hurting students or having to face them again. In addition, some faculty indicated censoring evaluations because they are part of a public record. (This was not always the case since at least Santa Cruz and Sarah Lawrence employed censors to examine evaluations before public exposure.) A small percentage of faculty at each college ran into one of two obstacles, resulting in a mechanical evaluation not different from grades. Either the graders found the written evaluations too difficult and sought to avoid them, or they were unable to deal with the paradigm of the C student. The major pitfalls were best illustrated by the small percentage of faculty at each school who said, "I just don't know what to write."

A faculty member must know his students well if he is to write a meaningful evaluation of their performance. Graders and students alike frequently indicated that evaluation is especially poor in large classes, with definitions of "large" ranging from ten to forty. And since large classes are most common in general education and early major courses, students are most likely to receive their poorest evaluations in their critical first two years. Some faculty, as mentioned, are unable to provide evaluations for middle-range inconspicuous students. When such evaluations are required, these professors provide only general, meaningless, and mechanical evaluations.

Evaluation forms themselves create large problems. At two schools evaluation forms have check boxes and four-by-one inch spaces for comments. Small numbers of faculty at each school indicated that they check the boxes but do not write comments in the space provided. These evaluations were often criticized for saying little. At several other schools a blank piece of paper is provided for faculty comments. These evaluations were criticized—by three institutional studies and by many administrators, faculty, and students—for their lack of uniformity and absence of norms in preparation. In each case, it was not uncommon for faculty to ask students to evaluate themselves; one third of all evaluations at Antioch were of this nature. As a result of this multimethod approach, administrators frequently complained that it is not possible to get an overall picture of many of the students. A similar problem occurs when faculty use evaluations neither as grades nor as supplements to grades, but rather to speak to an individual student. A poor student may be commended for his hard work, while an A student may be told that he lacks initiative. As such, evaluations lose any public value they may have. At some schools grades are combined with written evaluations; letter grades are supposed to represent a student's standing in comparison with peers, and evaluations represent comparisons with a student's own potential. Students, however, frequently viewed the effect as a lack of coordination between grades and evaluations. To prevent this misunderstanding and the associated problems of multimethod evaluations, the purpose and format of evaluations must be made clear to the entire college community.

Institutional studies at Antioch, Wesleyan, and the Residential College at the University of Michigan urged greater faculty commitment to evaluations. Student opinions about faculty seriousness varied considerably at all ten schools, with students most negative at Brown and most positive at Antioch and Sarah Lawrence. Similarly, at Sarah Lawrence the entire faculty with one exception viewed the evaluations positively, and at Brown most of the faculty viewed the evaluations negatively. As a result of faculty attitudes and similar administrative views, evaluations are far more seriously regarded at Sarah Lawrence. At Brown, a few faculty said that they personally discouraged student evaluation requests.

School size often determines the success of an evaluation system. Evaluations were viewed far more positively at the schools with smaller student-faculty ratios and greater student-faculty contact time, since these schools have increased student-faculty interaction. This explains why evaluations were regarded so poorly at Brown, a large school with less than average student-faculty contact time. At the smaller schools, however, evaluations were sometimes criticized for repeating what faculty had already told the students. At schools like Santa Cruz, where size increases are planned in the next few years, evaluations will probably become poorer in quality and less frequent in number. As one Santa Cruz professor said, "The written evaluation system is a good way to begin a school, but it cannot be sustained after the school becomes increasingly complex."

Evaluations apparently make little difference in school environment or student performance. The only comments recorded consistently, though in small numbers, were that evaluations did result in a diminution of pressure and provided a more personalized touch. On the other hand, students indicated difficulty in obtaining evaluations from their instructors and complained that evaluations were usually late. The lateness results, at least in part, from the additional time required to write the evaluations.

At Santa Cruz and Brown particularly, many students readily admitted little interest in their evaluations, saying that they had not seen them in several semesters, if at all. At Brown, where students must request evaluations, faculty complained that students request evaluations in only those courses where they performed well. Similarly, cases of "evaluation grubbing" were cited at two other schools. Finally, evaluations are more expensive than a letter or numerical grading system. The exact differential has not been computed at any sample school, though institutional research at Antioch indicated that the cost difference is great. One indication may come from Evergreen State College in Olympia, Washington, which charges the student ten dollars for each copy of his transcript; the transcript includes evaluations by both the student and faculty members and representative samples of the student's work.

Oral Evaluations

Oral evaluations, examined at St. John's, present—in intensified form—many of the problems found with written evaluations. Most notably there was an enhanced level of politeness and lack of candor, imposed in part by the fear of unnecessary cruelty to students but also by the evaluation format of face-to-face confrontation. In addition, faculty must spend even more time preparing and delivering oral evaluations than is required for written evaluations, simply by virtue of the formal sessions required.

The St. John's "don rag" (evaluation session) was often criticized for its discontinuity with grades; and most instructors admitted that they use the sessions to evaluate each student according to his own ability. Thus, a C student might be praised for giving his all, and an A student might be criticized for "slacking off." In addition, since St. John's is a small school with close contact between students and faculty, many complained that the evaluation sessions simply repeated the informal student-faculty sessions. As a result, the senior session has now been eliminated, and there is serious talk of eliminating the junior session as well.

But in spite of these problems, the oral evaluation has several distinct advantages. It is especially helpful for the shy student, since it forces him to meet with all of his instructors at regular intervals. According to instructors, these meetings frequently resulted in follow-up dialogue between such students and the instructor. Moreover, because the St. John's evaluation takes place in the presence of students and colleagues, the evaluating instructor considers his job more seriously than the author of written evaluations. The one-sentence evaluation is no longer possible, nor is omission of evaluations for the average student.

Covert Grades

Covert grading—letter-graded systems employed only for external use and created with the purpose of denying or discouraging student knowledge of grades—was examined at four schools: Reed, Prescott, Sarah Lawrence, and St. John's. The rationale for covert grades is to deemphasize grades in order to redirect student interest to learning. Elimination of overt grades was intended to minimize the anxiety and competition associated with traditional grading. Anxiety due to student ignorance of grades was not expected, since all systems notify students when doing poorly.

The most notable fact about covert grading systems is that they fail to be covert. At Reed 83 percent, at Prescott 25 percent, at St. John's 36 percent, and at Sarah Lawrence 48 percent of the students interviewed had knowledge of their grades. These percentages may be significantly lower than the actual percentage of students who knew their grades, since there is a stigma attached to asking for grades. During the interviews, students were clearly embarrassed when admitting they had asked for grades, and in group interviews peers would react adversely when one or more of their number admitted such knowledge. The large divergence in the percentages is accounted for by several factors. Of the four schools, Reed is the only one that does not provide additional feedback mechanisms. Each of the other schools has an oral or a written evaluation, and Prescott even supplements the evaluation with an honors/satisfactory/fail designation. As a result, the Reed student receives the least evaluative information, and the Prescott student receives the most. In addition, a larger percentage of Reed students attend graduate school than do the students from the other colleges; consequently, the Reed students are under greater pressure to ascertain their grades. Finally, Reed has by far the most difficult entrance requirements, and its students tend to be high achievers from largely grade-oriented systems. It should therefore not be surprising that half of the Reed students felt a high degree of anxiety over grades, a level much higher than that expressed at the other schools.

At Reed the faculty members interviewed said that they did tell anxious students their grades—either directly or with codes used to maintain the covert veneer; for example, an A student might be told that he did "exceptionally," and a B student might be told that his grade was "above average." Similarly, at the other schools the vast majority of faculty said that they would tell students their grades, though in general not as obliquely as at Reed. At Sarah Lawrence, one administrator said that more students are coming to see their grades every year. Many interviewees at each of the schools used the expression "hypocritical," though it was not suggested by interviewers. There appears to be, then, a high level of dissatisfaction with covert grading, though this dissatisfaction may be based simply on ideology. That is, since the covertness in grading exists mostly in theory, so may the criticism directed against it.

Pass/Fail and Credit/No Credit Systems

Credit/no credit differs from pass/fail in that credit/no credit does not record failing grades on the student's public record. All the total pass/fail and credit/no credit systems observed have additional feedback components as well (for instance, written evaluations used at Santa Cruz), and the pass/fail system was viewed as insignificant when compared with the additional mechanisms. Comments regarding credit/no credit in no way distinguished it from pass/fail. Since failure has become infrequent, the idea of not recording failure was seen to make little difference. However, a small number of students, usually well under a fifth, said that they would have preferred grades. Individuals accurately characterized the system as permitting greater freedom for the motivated students and permitting the nonmotivated students to flounder. In general, however, interviewees did admit that pass/fail systems do diminish pressure.

Many of the schools in our study have instituted variations of the total pass/fail system: four-point pass/fail systems, three-point systems, partial pass/fail systems, pass/fail in special programs, and pass/fail for the first year or two.

Four-point pass/fail. Four-point pass/fail systems (honors/ high pass/pass/fail) were examined at Yale and Bowdoin. According to students and faculty, the four-point system at these two colleges is much the same in practice as A/B/C/F grading systems. There has, as yet, been no detailed evaluation of the Bowdoin system, but at Yale the grades are highly inflated. Faculty and students alike indicated that "pass" has become a poor grade. "Pass" accounts for only one quarter of Yale's grades; almost 75 percent of the grades are either "high pass" or "honors." Until 1972, when the "fail" category was eliminated at Yale, only about 1 percent of the grades were "fail"—indicating that D's had been absorbed in "pass."

At Bowdoin, students and faculty greeted the four-point system neutrally, finding little if any difference from the twelve-point system abandoned in 1967. At Yale, where the transition from a numerical system occurred in 1967, the faculty were not enthusiastic either.

Three-point grading. Three-point grading systems were examined at Prescott and Eckerd. Although both colleges use the honors/pass/fail system, each employs supplementary written evaluations. A plurality of faculty and student interviewees responded positively to the three-point system, but most opinions were negative or neutral. The most significant problem is that the definition of "honors" is not clear. At Prescott, which uses the system only for internal purposes, "honors" is granted for "sustained and exceptional scholarship"; at Eckerd "honors" is granted for "work distinctly above average." These are the clearest guidelines available. At Prescott most faculty rarely give "honors," some give "honors" as frequently as they would an A, and others never give it. Individual professors at Eckerd vary widely in their practices, but the school-wide average for "honors" grades is 30 percent. An increase in the number of "honors" grades given at Eckerd has been noted over the past few years.

Not too surprisingly, both students and faculty at Prescott and Eckerd described the three-point grading system as "arbitrary." They also complained that the system, especially the "pass" designation, is too vague. A few students objected to a "pass" grade as insufficient reward for an almost "honors" student. Several faculty said that they are unable to distinguish adequately between middle-range students. One professor felt that the grading system enhances mediocrity. In addition, graduate schools, especially medical schools utilizing central admissions services, commonly translate the "pass" as a C when evaluating the student transcripts. This method severely handicaps the almost "honors" student.

Solutions to the problems posed are not easy. Three-point grading systems are initiated to deemphasize grades; therefore, providing fixed percentages of "honors," "pass," and "fail" grades would work against this goal. Establishing additional work as the only criterion for "honors" would still not distinguish the excellent "pass" student in graduate admissions. These were the most commonly advanced alternatives, with the exception of eliminating "honors," which was suggested by one third of the Eckerd faculty.

Partial pass/fail systems.   Programs permitting students to take a given number of courses pass/fail were examined at Brandeis, Brown, Trinity, and the Residential College at the University of Michigan.

About half of the students interviewed said that they used the pass/fail system primarily to avoid hurting their cumulative averages or to take courses they ordinarily would avoid. A smaller number said that they used pass/fail to obtain a specific desired knowledge—often focusing on only a portion of a non-major course—or to secure a course with no work. A study of grading at Brandeis by Dean of Admissions Matthew Sgan (1970) indicates that most students use pass/fail to meet general education requirements.

Most of the students interviewed said either that they worked less than usual in their pass/fail courses or that they performed as they usually did; a much smaller number said that their performance was better in pass/fail courses. The Sgan study showed that for freshmen, sophomores, and juniors in pass/fail courses (using letter grades submitted by instructors for pass/fail students) average grades were significantly lower than were those given in non-pass/fail courses. Although this study may indicate only that students take courses pass/fail in their weaker areas, it is compatible with other indications that they do slack off.

Accompanying partial pass/fail systems is an unplanned increase in emphasis on concentration. At Brown nearly half of the sample specifically took pass/fail courses only outside their major; at Brandeis and Trinity pass/fail courses are not permitted in the major. In view of the slacking off in pass/fail courses which are generally taken outside the major and the admission by students of greater emphasis on graded courses, students are obtaining a greater major orientation at the cost of general education.

Student participation in the pass/fail system has been high at each of the schools. At Trinity, which permits one pass/fail course each semester, the average student graduates with five or six pass/fails. At Brown, where a student may specify any number of courses pass/fail, 85 percent of the students participate each year, in numbers decreasing by class—freshmen most, seniors least; however, the absolute number of pass/fails each year has decreased by about one sixth over three terms (possibly because students have come to recognize the risk involved in the large-scale use of pass/fail). At Brandeis, where four pass/fails are permitted, with a one-per-term maximum, slightly over half of the seniors participate; however, unlike Brown, the percentages increase for each class. At the Residential College the number of pass/fails permitted and the nature of the system are still in flux, but participation is high. The only exception to the large-scale student use of pass/fail occurred at the University of Wisconsin at Green Bay (UWGB). Only 238 pass/fails had been chosen by 215 of the 4000 students in attendance in a system which permits almost unlimited use of the pass/fail option. The reasons for the lack of use are not clear, though many of the students are first-generation college students and highly grade and job oriented.

Special programs pass/fail. The Experimental College Program, the two-year Berkeley program occupying from two thirds to all of a student's freshman and sophomore schedule, and the Harvard freshman-seminar program, a one-semester freshman course, were the special programs examined. Both utilize pass/fail grading. These two programs are similar in that their admissions rely upon student self-selection, a process whereby a student volunteers to be part of a program.

The pass/fail system was criticized by none of the Experimental College program faculty and only one of the freshman-seminar faculty. Students at both Berkeley and Harvard favored the grading system approximately three to one. Very few Harvard students felt that they had performed less well in their ungraded seminar than in their graded courses. In both programs the freedom and lack of pressure provided were frequently mentioned. In addition, "creative" and other such adjectives were applied more frequently than to other programs.

Self-selection is the key to the greater success noted in pass/fail grading in special programs. Students in these programs were not forced to seek refuge in external sources for the motivation they lacked for their work, as was the case in some other programs examined.

Pass/Fail for First Year or Two.   Two schools examined, Haverford and the California Institute of Technology (Cal. Tech.), employ grading systems which distinguish between the early and later years of college. Until 1972 Haverford generally used pass/fail for the first two years, although letter grades were recorded and, in the major field, occasionally released to graduate schools. By 1972 Haverford had abandoned pass/fail and was giving and releasing letter grades in virtually all courses. Cal. Tech. gives all pass/fail grades for the freshman year.

The differences in the employment of the grading systems at the two schools were profound merely because Haverford released some grades. Cal. Tech. does not make this concession—and does not need to, because it is recognized as the most prestigious science-oriented college in the country, with one of the two or three most able student bodies (Cass and Birnbaum, 1970–1971). Haverford's release of selected grades, in practice, created a partial pass/fail system outside the student's major. As a result, the weaknesses of partial pass/fail grading accrued to Haverford's freshman and sophomore grading system, including an enhanced emphasis upon concentration, since this is all that "counts." Only about one seventh of the students interviewed, many planning to attend professional school, felt that their pass/fail grades "counted."

Largely because of the college's intense academic pressure, pass/fail makes a significant difference to many freshmen at Cal. Tech. Over half the students interviewed felt that the system gave them a chance to adjust socially and/or academically; about one seventh would have preferred grades, and another seventh said that because they were not graded, they had been free to emphasize their more important major courses. Students entering Cal. Tech. already have a predilection toward the sciences, so that further removal from the social sciences and humanities is a serious problem. One third of the students indicated that the pass/fail freshman year had caused them to slack off; an equal number felt that they had gained more from their studies. Nonetheless, a 1970 institutional research study which contrasted matched student samples before and after the 1964 grading change, found no significant differences in cumulative averages, Graduate Record Examination scores, attrition, or major choice; and few students felt any difficulty adapting to sophomore-year grading. In general, students and faculty strongly approved of pass/fail grading in the freshman year. The greatest weakness is the failure to compensate for the absence of grades by providing students with other information regarding the quality of their performances.

Graduate Schools and Grading Systems

Graduate and particularly professional schools are the chief obstacle in the way of grading change. While undergraduate colleges are turning toward individual and nontraditional evaluations, the graduate schools—particularly the medical schools—are demanding uniform and easily codeable grading systems, letter or numerical.

In a 1970 study conducted by Yale, four hundred graduate deans and department chairmen were asked whether the abolition of the F grade in the four-point grading system (a change later adopted at Yale) would have negative effects on the Yale student applying to graduate school. Two hundred responses were received from twenty-three schools—five "ivy league" schools, ten state universities, and eight other schools—all considered prestigious. Most of the graduate deans (54 percent) indicated possible negative effects. In our own interviews, numerous registrars, deans of students, and graduate school counselors spoke of experiences paralleling those predicted by the Yale study. Somewhat similarly, Schoemer, Thomas, and Bragonier (1973) found that "once a student records 10 percent or more nontraditional grades, his chances for admission and financial support are jeopardized." Any abberations from traditional letter or numerical grades severely hurt the middle-range student, particularly in professional school admissions. The excellent student generally does not suffer, since his empty transcript is supplemented by high scores on the Graduate Record Examination and impressive recommendations.

At the twenty sample schools, with four explainable exceptions, a clear pattern was observed: traditional grades accompanied by no graduate school difficulties, or nontraditional grades accompanied by graduate school difficulties. The deviations are consistent with the paradigm presented. Reed has experienced difficulties, according to the registrar, because of its grading guidelines, which produce cumulative averages significantly lower than the inflated averages of other schools. The difficulty occurs despite Reed's computation of cumulative averages and class rank. Cal. Tech. and New College experience no difficulty because of the exceedingly high Graduate Record Examination scores of their students. Cal. Tech. students average in the 91 percentile verbally and the 95 quantitatively; New College students average in the 98 percentile. Although their students may, in principle, be handicapped by an absence of grades, they more than compensate for the lack of grades with Graduate Record Examination scores. The problems of pass/ fail grading at the Experimental College Program at Berkeley were overcome by flexibility and small size. Files on each student were maintained, and the faculty knew each student well; consequently, grading difficulties could be remedied by written recommendations, and grades could be provided if absolutely necessary. Furthermore, no concentration preparation occurred in the Experimental College Program; rather, the entire major program was pursued in the letter-graded Berkeley College of Arts and Letters.

The problems created by graduate schools offer little promise of prompt resolution. Even at those universities with nontraditional grading systems at the undergraduate level, many administrators and faculty refuse to change admissions policies at their own graduate and professional schools. The University of Michigan medical school, for example, will not accept written evaluations from the Residential College; the law school, in contrast, will accept the evaluations but will not promise to read them. Similarly, many graduate departments at Brown will not consider pass/fail-graded Brown students.

Graduate school admissions, a seller's market, has caused several schools to initiate changes in their grading structure designed to help students. Santa Cruz permits students the option of electing letter grades in basic science courses, a concession for medical school applicants. Haverford, before it ended freshman pass/fail grading altogether, sometimes permitted students to send their major grades earned during the pass/fail freshman and sophomore years to graduate school. These concessions had deleterious effects on the grading systems at both schools. Another school has even translated evaluations into grades in order to help some of its students. At Brown more than half of the student sample unsolicitedly expressed graduate school apprehension, citing it as the rationale for their use of the grading system. An almost equal portion of the faculty indicated concern over graduate school reaction to the grading system. The result of these fears has been a dramatic decrease in the use of pass/fail at Brown, and this behavior was mirrored at all sample schools with pass/fail options.

Recommendation

In view of the multitude of weaknesses indicated in all sample evaluation systems, we clearly did not find an ideal grading method. Therefore, we propose that a dual system be considered. This system would consist of letter grades for both external and internal use and modified written evaluations for internal use only. Admittedly, letter grading is one of the poorest of all grading systems. It suffers from diversity in meaning, capriciousness, lack of consideration in handling, highly inflated distributions, and a very high degree of subjectivity. However, graduate and professional schools want letter grades. And any university that adopts a nontraditional system of evaluation is reducing its students' chances of acceptance into graduate or professional schools. We therefore recommend that letter grades be maintained—but only until a sizable number of colleges can get together and agree that they all will adopt alternate grading practices. In view of the greater value and degree of success of several of the other grading systems, some such agreement seems imperative. In the meantime, the letter grades used should be clearly defined, translatable into a system meaningful to students, faculty, and administrators.

Written evaluations, though methodologically and structurally weak, apparently provide the greatest degree of individual feedback. Therefore, we recommend that a modified system of written evaluations be used only within the college, since many faculty will tone down their evaluations if they are to be used outside the college. In addition, evaluation systems are costly when maintained for outside use and are too bulky and diffuse to be of value to graduate schools. Copies of the evaluation, then, would be sent only to the student, the specific faculty instructor, and the student's advisor. No university record of evaluations would be maintained.

The evaluation itself would consist of the student's self-evaluation and an instructor's evaluation. The evaluation process would begin with the student's submitting a self-evaluation explaining what he did in the course (specifically describing readings, projects, discussions, and other relevant material); what he thinks about his own performance and about the course itself; and what follow-up plans, if any, he has relating to the course. Faculty evaluations would ideally discuss the student's evaluation and include additional comments; at the very least, they would serve to rationalize the grades given by faculty members. Such evaluations would be mandatory for students during the freshman year, during periods of academic probation, and whenever requested by a professor or a student. In the case of an evaluation initiated by the professor, the requirement would be as any other requirement in a course, so that students would have to prepare the self-evaluation necessary to get the ball rolling. A student initiating an evaluation would be required, by a date set early in the term, to inform the professor of his intent to seek an evaluation.

This model permits students and faculty to assemble a collected dossier of the student's performance, and also for faculty members to obtain feedback on their teaching and course quality. Moreover, such a system is necessary for students, who, in each segment of this study, exhibited little initiative or thought regarding their education. The self-evaluation would force them to begin to think about their studies. In addition, the student's self-evaluation informs the faculty member of the areas about which the student is concerned, thus giving the faculty member a framework in which to structure his comments. Self-evaluations of this nature were highly praised by students made to write them at Haverford for the Freshman Inquiry (see Chapter Two). Even if this method is no more successful than the current written-evaluation systems, which is unlikely because of the several improvements suggested, the system would still be a valuable addition to the letter grades.

The only remaining disadvantage would be cost. While the cost of maintenance would be eliminated, the minor cost of printing, and the less minor cost of faculty time would remain. Since the system is required only for one year, however, the amount of faculty time ultimately would be reduced and more purposefully utilized.

Toward a Reformation of Undergraduate Education

𑁋𑁋𑁋𑁋𑁋𑁋𑁋𑁋𑁋𑁋𑁋𑁋𑁋𑁋𑁋𐎜𐎜𐎜𐎜𐎜𐎜𐎜𐎜𐎜𐎜𐎜𐎜𐎜

Consistent patterns of student, faculty, and administrative behavior emerge from discussion of each curriculum structure. This chapter describes those patterns, identifies several needs, and points out problems and potential solutions.

Student Character

Perhaps because traditional job opportunities and life styles are being questioned by many, an increasing lack of direction among college students has appeared in recent years. The interviewers repeatedly met students who said they had no idea what they wanted or why they were in college, and the dramatic rise in attrition and drop in immediate pursuit of graduate school show the comments to be more than rhetorical.

Although some students—mainly those interested in a specific profession or field of study—did attempt to plan coherent programs, the others—the majority—wandered from term to term, usually seeking the path of least "hassle." While the resounding reply of faculty and administrators to this situation has been "Improve the advising system!" substantial portions of the student body at each school said flatly that they had no interest in using advisors, regardless of the accessibility or knowledge of such advisors. Similarly, at schools utilizing written evaluations, students were not sufficiently interested to obtain faculty appraisals. On the whole, students did not express their lack of interest arrogantly; they simply felt that they were aware of all the alternatives and merely had to choose the least objectionable courses, major, graduate school, or career.

We did not specifically seek "student leaders" because we felt from our own experience that such students tend to dramatize the intensity of their constituents' dissatisfaction. Nevertheless, interviews with student body presidents were arranged by several colleges, and a few other student leaders were found through the random-selection interview process. Most of them told of great student interest in a different grading system, revised requirements, and the addition of nondepartmental options. The other students interviewed indicated that these student leaders were not misrepresenting the direction but only the magnitude of student thought. Most students, when asked specifically about an issue mentioned by a student leader, agreed with his or her diagnosis, but few were as concerned with it. This helps explain why programs that are established at some schools presumably because of student pressure and initiative then are undersubscribed.

Students were not well aware of the curricular opportunities available to them. When asked whether they had considered creating their own major, many were amazed that such a possibility existed, and substantial numbers of students at several schools supplied the interviewers with misinformation. Even when a program was well used and considered successful, students emphasized fewer of the philosophic attributes than did the faculty. For example, faculty members said that the freshman seminars made an important contribution to the student's first year and helped him to choose a major; students minimized the former and discounted the latter. Similarly, professors at Bowdoin praised the senior seminars for exposing students to a new field; yet this factor was cited by only one member of the student sample.

Another noteworthy sidelight observed in all seminar programs was that some faculty sought to offer "relevant" courses, primarily because they thought that was what students wanted. Yet students, in class enrollments as well as interviews, exhibited no specific commitment to such courses; in fact, the word "relevant" was used frequently and exclusively by faculty interviewees. This attempted bribing of students is related to a feeling expressed by several students at some of the more "liberal" colleges—namely, that faculty are afraid of students. At Santa Cruz students told of professors who assigned books, papers, and topics of study, and then backed down when students complained. This behavior could, of course, be viewed as a healthy responsiveness to class members; but the students made clear that the faculty action came from a desire to be popular and often resulted in semester-long, contentless bull sessions.

A larger problem raised at many schools was the need of students to be told exactly what to do. According to the directors of seminar programs that offer several courses with open topics, the students enrolled are unable to participate actively in the creation of a seminar topic and format. Exasperated professors complained that they eventually had to pick a topic themselves and at Trinity seven of the eight instructors interviewed who had offered seminars with open topics said it was not worth trying again. Teachers of all types of courses, both in and out of departments, recounted the experience of loosening the definition and limits of a course to provide for student initiative only to have to return to personal domination when no student interest or response was registered. Similarly, students in the Experimental College Program at Berkeley were unable to cope with the weekly leaderless meeting of a seminar which alternately met with a professor and/or graduate student. The need to be told what to do was apparent in student practices regarding curricular opinions. Students were consistently willing to enroll in nondepartmental courses; but, even though opportunities were available, they were not inclined to take the initiative to design a course or an independent-study program.

The student numbness should not be surprising. Students were observers in grade school. They only watched the teacher; they could react only when the teacher told them to react, or they were abused: "Only babies speak out; adults raise their hands and wait to be called on." When they answered a question incorrectly, the teacher often scorned them and the class laughed. After a few unpleasantries they learned to keep quiet and wait to be told what to do. Most sadly the eager inquisitive gleam in the child's eye disappeared by the time he or she entered college. So when the college said to the student, "Boy, do we have a program for you," the student sat back and waited to be told what to do.

A suitable college program should put increasing responsibility in the student's hands for his education. Initially college students are new and need time to adjust, so that requiring all students to plan their freshman year would be traumatic. However, when students are required to design their own majors, they are forced to think about what they are doing and where they are going. Even if—as 50 percent of the Justin Morrill students did—they eventually choose to construct standard departmental majors, they are at least forced to rationalize their program and course choices. Students at Haverford highly praised the Inquiry program, which requires that each student assess his performance and future plans. In addition, required independent and field study help to break the traditional ritual. These programs, which foster independent learning, point to the path that colleges should be following. The specific programs a college adopts should be tailored to the student body and the purpose of the institution.

Faculty Character

Higher education is one of the most carefully groomed family businesses in America. Each potential faculty member ordinarily spends seven years of apprenticeship as an undergraduate and a graduate student, scrutinizing his future profession and learning the ropes of the trade. Existing faculty then pass upon the apprentice's acceptability. But even if a few rotten apples are chosen, the old-timers still have discretionary powers of reappointment and tenure at one-, three-, and six-year intervals. In short, faculty have the power to define qualifications, standards, and responsibilities for their own jobs. And graduate schools are the real meat of the system. They are the finishing schools for all future faculty, where the money goes and where the prestige comes from.

Graduate schools emphasize research and specialty. Graduate students learn quickly that a great teacher who devotes endless time to his students will be known by no one but the students on one campus. The professor seeking a name must reach more people than could fit into the largest lecture hall. An article or book not only has the potential to reach millions of people, but more important, it can reach someone of professional value who might remember the author's name, publicly quote him, praise his article, or help him in the future. Keeping up with the literature is the name applied to finding out where the competition and the money are. Therefore, graduate school faculties concentrate on doing research instead of teaching—carving out a specialty fiefdom and commanding government and foundation monies. If a graduate school has "big-name" professors who bring big money to their departments, that school is considered a high-powered institution; and high-powered institutions bring in more money, more graduate students, and more "big names." When there is a graduate school on campus, faculty move in the graduate school direction. Columbia has gone as far as separating the offices of the general education Contemporary Civilization faculty from their departments. Moreover, creation of a graduate school is a tremendous drain on university funds. It reinforces standard departmental structures, eats up faculty time, and lessens the emphasis upon the undergraduate college.

Because of their influence and power, graduate schools succeed in establishing the norms for all undergraduate education. Undergraduate institutions follow the standards desired by the graduate school because even the smallest deviations have meant that students were refused entrance. Even when colleges do not follow graduate school guidelines, the students do on their own. The case for graduate school domination was well documented in our discussion of divergent grading practices (see Chapter Eight). In their conservatism and professionalism, graduate schools have done all possible to stifle any real change and experimentation in undergraduate education.

The faculty sample who chose to work in colleges without graduate schools did so because of their lack of research emphasis and associated competition. Although individuals missed specific features of the university, such as laboratories, more colleagues, graduate students (to provide inexpensive teaching and thereby reduce the cost of staffing), and a better library, the most serious disadvantages were in the natural sciences, where several instructors had to shift their emphasis to history or philosophy of science due to the lack of facilities and time to engage in pure research.

Since faculty members have created the rules, they know that potential professors must be experts in some field. This means that students who are the professors of tomorrow must be encouraged to specialize as early as possible. Even the interdisciplinary general education programs are made up of individual departmental courses which are required for concentration by the sponsoring department. Graduate programs are strictly divided along departmental lines, so that a student will spend three or more years with people interested in only one field. Thus, faculty members who do not seek a Ph.D., signifying competence in a specialty, go eventually to what are considered "the offbeat colleges that do not ask for a Ph.D." (Riesman, Gusfield, and Gamson, 1970, p. 8), if they can get jobs at all.

At the same time, the need to "make it" through one's specialty causes faculty members to view their discipline as more important than the college that pays their salary. A professor is a sociologist first and a faculty member at Bland College second; hence, institutional loyalty is low. Academic freedom, which has historically meant freedom from persecution for minority views, now implies the freedom to do one's research without interference. As the number of students attending college and student-faculty ratios have grown, the number of courses each professor teaches has shrunk; yet even the small current course load is often considered an infringement upon faculty time. However, most faculty members, despite large differences in student contact time demanded of them at the twenty-six colleges, responded similarly when asked if they had enough time by saying they could always use more but the problem wasn't serious.

Nevertheless, if the need to publish new research is taken as a given, the amount of work for each faculty member cannot be sneezed at. Particularly noteworthy, because it is so insidious, is the amount of time absorbed by committee work. Despite the low faculty institutional loyalty, faculty members have a fear of being left out as they were historically, so that they insist on serving on committees as trivial as student housing, parking, or dining. Because of faculty distrust of administrators, and their desire to avoid further dividing an already tight university budget by hiring new ones, educational programs are increasingly governed by committee. The proliferation of committees has reached the stage where it cuts deeply into the time that could be spent on research or teaching. Faculty are now approaching the point where many are tired of committees and want to be left alone.

Many professors at the twenty-six schools considered their function to be teaching their specialty to those who might pursue it. Thus, core courses and other nondepartmental offerings generally received no faculty support. Such programs are approved by faculty because a few zealous or romantic individuals, occasionally backed by "responsible student leaders," are convinced that the programs will not hurt them and are even morally defensible. A favorable vote means being a good guy and entails no responsibility to do more than cynically observe.

Those professors who do participate in nondepartmental programs are often incapable of doing so successfully. Because they are trained to be specialists, they have difficulty teaching interdisciplinary courses; and, perhaps because they have been taught to view themselves as independent professionals, they are unable to work together. Faculty indifference and incompetence have been largely responsible for the failure of core and team-taught programs. Proponents and staffers of interdisciplinary programs consistently spoke of the difficulty in attracting and organizing a core faculty. Core staff members were frequently forced to participate; possibly for that reason, they attended staff meetings reluctantly and sporadically and never thought of attending a colleague's lectures and courses. The latter phenomenon was observed in every school except

St. John's and the Experimental College Program, where faculty had the peculiar notion that they could learn as well as teach. Academic freedom has come to mean also the right to teach in strict privacy.

Interdisciplinary seminar programs experienced similar problems because they, unlike core courses, are generally optional for students and no set number of offerings is required. Faculty therefore are not pressured into participating, and few courses are offered. Faculty indifference frequently harms the quality as well as the quantity of these courses. Interdisciplinary programs are rarely attractive to faculty members because such programs threaten to remove them from the arena where they can gain fame and fortune. Since most faculty hiring revolves about the departments, there is no opportunity for a college to specifically bring in faculty who have had experience either as students or teachers within the core programs. Department chairmen strive to protect their department members by keeping them entirely within the department.

Faculty inability to work together was the major weakness found even in special programs. Professors teaching in Directed Studies at Yale indicated that the absence of an integrated approach to learning, due to isolated departmental staffing, is the program's major failing. Even more surprising was the consensus that the two cycles of faculty in Berkeley's Experimental College Program, all of whom had volunteered, had been unable to work together satisfactorily.

Faculty members consistently exhibited an ignorance of the curricular offerings available at their school. Knowledge of interdisciplinary study opportunities, as well as programs available at other schools, was particularly lacking. Though most faculty members said they knew where to refer students who specifically asked about options and offerings outside the departments, the fact that such programs were unfamiliar to them severely limited their competence as advisors.

Clearly, faculty members are not an evil group of people. We live in a society which demands experts in highly specialized areas. So a potential answer lies not in chastising the faculty member for his poor behavior but in changing the society or subverting the rewards it offers.

Five possible solutions can be suggested. One way is to change faculty character by changing the criteria for salary increment and promotion. For example, instead of conducting faculty honors on the basis of publish or perish, a school could substitute a teach-and-prosper orientation, which requires that professors spend their time with their students. At Antioch, Bard, Prescott, Santa Cruz, and Sarah Lawrence an emphasis was placed on closer student-faculty relations. The outcome was most successful at Sarah Lawrence, where, under the presidency of Harold Taylor, faculty were told that their obligation was simply to teach. If individuals wanted, they could write and publish on their own time. On the other hand, the Santa Cruz administration tried to increase student-faculty contact in the creation of their own university; however, tenure is the responsibility of the larger University of California, which uses traditional criteria in evaluation. The result at Santa Cruz is a somewhat higher level of student-faculty contact than at many universities but certainly not the level anticipated and not at all comparable to that at Sarah Lawrence.

The difference in what happened at Santa Cruz and Sarah Lawrence is the result of clear operating criteria. Sarah Lawrence issued an unabstruse statement showing exactly how the bread would be buttered, and lived up to it. If a persuasive case is not made by a dissenting school, then it makes good sense for a faculty member to do what comes naturally.

If a criteria change is successful, the result will be a new kind of faculty—high personal-contact time, low publication rate. Most schools are unwilling to accept this as desirable; rather, they would prefer the outcome of the Santa Cruz effort—slightly better contact, relatively high publication. This requires only lip service and an occasional tenure award to a good teacher lacking in publications. Doing this maintains things as they are but somewhat increases faculty interest in students, since there is an outside chance that this extra activity might be a deciding factor later. Even if a faculty member is willing to sponsor more independent-study courses when teaching is a criterion for advancement, it is highly unlikely that he will teach additional courses. Therein lies the chief limitation of criteria change. It offers no acceptable middle road, only extremes, in that teaching and research are conflicting activities, both demanding a big allocation of time. To concentrate on one is to sacrifice the other, and to attempt both is, for most, to do a mediocre job at each. No university wants the mediocre staff which a balanced criteria program produces, so that the alternative for most universities is to stress either research or teaching.

A second possible solution to the faculty-attitude problem is to provide cash incentives for teaching general education courses. This method admittedly is expensive and fails to change faculty character, but it does succeed in producing new faculty teaching patterns. The nature of the incentive must be planned so that it does succeed in attracting faculty. For instance, the Columbia Chamberlain Fellowship for teaching Contemporary Civilization, which offers a sabbatical after three years, does not attract faculty, but only encourages them not to leave after two and a half years. Stanford and Harvard use cash incentives to attract faculty to their freshman-seminar programs. As a result, unlike the Brown Modes of Thought program, there is an equitable distribution of freshman seminars at Stanford and Harvard. However, the cost of the Stanford program is $79,000 and the Harvard program $100,000. As a result of money limitations, neither school is able to mount sufficient seminars for its entire freshman class. At Harvard nearly the whole freshman class applies for a seminar; yet only one third can be accommodated. Moreover, when cash incentives are offered to some, faculty with light teaching loads and their departments become reticent to teach without pay. However, if money is not a problem, which is doubtful at any American school, cash incentives provide an instant flexibility. For example, Stanford, responding to increased student demand, mounted twenty-one additional seminars in one year, increasing from sixty-four to eighty-five seminars, while Trinity was unable to produce even the thirty-nine needed seminars.

Two other methods for changing faculty character are geographical reshuffling and increasing teaching loads. Geographical reshuffling of faculty offices provides an immediately impotent, though possibly long-range, effective solution, while increasing teaching loads provides a long-range ineffective solution with short-range potency.

Faculties are usually grouped together geographically by department; such groupings preserve the professional isolation and cause a heightened sense of departmental importance. All faculty at Santa Cruz, with the exception of those in the natural sciences, receive randomly assigned offices. Despite the failure in the sciences, the Santa Cruz administration felt that geographic reshuffling of offices contributed to additional interdisciplinary teaching and brought faculty from diverse fields together. Creation of interdisciplinary departments is a variation on the same theme, designed for the same purpose and used at Prescott and UWGB with results similar to Santa Cruz. This method, however, is unlikely to produce changes in individual professors. Although personal contact between people in different departments is enhanced, it is a big step from that to collaborating professionally, and even a larger step to sharing knowledge and working together. In addition, extra staff meetings and additional secretarial time are required to counter the lack of central informal contacts.

Another free method is to increase or redirect the faculty teaching load. Colleges can do this with moral impunity because of the low faculty teaching loads; they can also get away with it now, in view of the surplus faculty supply. None of the schools in the study attempted this method on either a grand scale or with more than a few isolated individuals since it is a dangerous step for an individual college. The more prized faculty will leave for more "reasonable" teaching loads elsewhere, and morale will be low among those remaining. Even more devasting is the prospect of a mass exodus if the employment situation changes.

One positive result is what occurred in Columbia's Contemporary Civilization, which a majority of the faculty were coerced into teaching. Many got to like the program and volunteered to teach again the following year. One person even decided to leave his specialty because he enjoyed teaching general courses and seeing the interrelationships of knowledge. People forced to teach freshman seminars frequently enjoyed their experience and many said they would like to do it again soon.

For colleges interested simply in creating more latitude in their programs, increasing the flexibility of departments is a last alternative. One of the major reasons for departmental inflexibility is the tenure system, which freezes faculty slots in areas where they are often unnecessary in future years, and often with faculty "stars" who fade after receiving their life appointment. One of the sample colleges did not employ tenure, in an attempt to achieve greater subject and faculty flexibility. Even though this school scorned the publish-or-perish orientation, some of its faculty felt an acute lack of job security and worked even harder on their research than ever, hoping to build a wad of research as security in case of sudden contract termination. In addition, the college had a very high faculty turnover rate, which is not surprising in view of increased faculty anxiety.

The elimination of tenure may not be a bad idea for all colleges, however. For instance, the president of that college recently said that the situation had been stabilized and that the high turnover rate was expected to drop rapidly. This college was new, experimental, isolated from any large city, and lacked accreditation, so that the deck was well stacked against it. Elimination of tenure would be far more realistic at an old, established, prestigious school, where faculty are begging to get in, or by a group of such colleges.

A less radical step involves forcing departments to fill slots in nondepartmental programs. This is the procedure followed at Columbia for the Contemporary Civilization program. To impose this kind of requirement upon a department is like increasing teaching loads in that it encourages people to look elsewhere for employment and makes the senior people feel that their department is being abused. However, if a college does attempt to make department personnel participate in nondepartmental programs, it should apply sufficient force so that it is taken seriously. At Trinity, where the administration actively supports the freshman-seminar program, the program director lacked sufficient clout to be able to make departments comply fully. Departments frequently gave him fewer faculty than he requested and thought they were doing him a favor. Another method involves breaking down departmental structures officially or on an ad hoc basis (see Chapter Six).

Administration Character

The university direction and leadership provided by the great college presidents—Gilman of Johns Hopkins, Harper and Hutchins of Chicago, Eliot of Harvard—have virtually disappeared. At the private college the president is a fund raiser; at the public university he is a political buffer. At Sarah Lawrence, for instance, several faculty complained that former president Harold Taylor had failed in his presidential role since he spent more time on the academy than on financing. And the rest of the administration performs a juggling act: trying to keep students, faculty, alumni, and the community quiet, costs low, and the university going. The leadership vacuum has been partially filled by faculty committees. The classic example is the Muscatine Committee at Berkeley; its report, *Education at Berkeley* (1968), received good coverage in the media —professional and nonprofessional. But the report was talked to death by the Berkeley faculty and had little impact upon the campus. Faculty leadership always fails in this manner, since faculty are a multidimensional group with many different, strongly ingrained ideas about what a university is and should be; at best, after hours of general faculty and committee consideration, they may emerge with a compromise that incorporates the opinions of the majority, but the result is more likely inaction. This process is sound politically but poor educationally. Noting the nature of this dilemma, William Buckley said, with regard to the 1968 Harvard Strike, that he would prefer to be governed by the first two hundred names in the Boston phonebook than by the Harvard faculty.

Students are becoming aware of this situation as well. In the early and middle 1960s students sought faculty support to fight what was perceived as an evil administration. Now they are beginning to understand that the problem rests with faculty and are aligning themselves with the administration. Though not completely successful, the Brown University curriculum reform is the first fruit of the student-administration coalition.

In fact, administration is the only source that can provide the needed academic leadership. Already the crescendo of jeers can be imagined: "Why, administrators—they haven't been in a classroom in years." And, of course, it is a liability for universities to hire professional administrators, individuals who lack experience with the personnel and environment comprising the university. It is also a liability to isolate administration from the rest of the university. For example, the executive vice-president at one of our sample schools knew so little about his university (for example, underestimating school size by over one third)` that interviewers were able to correct and inform him on the basic conditions of his institution. The proper administrator is an individual who is well acquainted with the particular institution, preferably having participated in it in a student or faculty role. Isolating administration is prevented by maintaining close contact between administrator and constituents. To encourage such contact and to regard it seriously is to create a healthy university responsive to the needs of its people. Similarly, it is an asset to have administrators who are not so conditioned by the classroom as to be unable to think beyond the course format. Students need to be made to think, and the closed, sterile classroom environment does not permit this. Future administrators must be able to see beyond the stifling traditional structures.

Administration alone has the tools to move a university— money and power. With these, administration has the ability to carry out an educationally sound and cohesive program. With these tools, the academic interests of faculty can be broadened. With these tools, departments can be broken up and alternative structures fostered. With these tools, administrators aided the formation of the Experimental College program at Berkeley while faculty committees all but prevented its institution. There is a wide world of possibilities if administrators would only take the first step, and ultimately this decision rests with the college president. The first step that should be taken is to provide an institutional philosophy at each college.

Need for Institutional Philosophy

Though the student dissent of the 1960s, which served as a catalyst for reassessment, has subsided, the far more pressing demands of the economic crunch felt by colleges remain as a stronger, more vital rationale for such collegiate reevaluation. Private colleges are being forced to find ways to diminish costs if they are to remain open. Public colleges also have to find ways to lower costs if they are to maintain their current size without undercutting their academic quality. As a result, much university reassessment, asking specifically how colleges can retain quality while cutting costs, is currently underway. The establishment of clearly defined university objectives and philosophies may be a desirable partial answer, since this method couples reduction of attrition with increased collegiate quality.

The external vagueness attributed to colleges goes hand in hand with an internal vagueness. As our study of curriculum structures has shown, undergraduate programs today lack curricular cohesion, and curriculum structures fail to meet stated objectives. These failings are largely the result of poorly formed curriculum ideals, based upon conflict avoidance and designed without cognizance of the realities of the university. For example, at the Residential College of the University of Michigan, most faculty members complained that the core curriculum does not meet their philosophical objectives for general education (Francis, 1970). It is a compromise curriculum—one that seriously offends no one but also represents no coherent curricular philosophy.

Once an institutional philosophy is articulated, specific curriculum structures mirroring that philosophy and fitted together in a cohesive fashion can be constructed, providing for a purposeful undergraduate program of education. Establishment of philosophically directed education is not consistent with denying students freedom. In fact, freedom could be the basis of the philosophy. This type of planning differs in its realization that four years of college is not an end but rather that education needs to have goals and a sense of purpose. After initiation of a philosophy has been accomplished, a degree becomes more than a Bachelor of Arts or Sciences. It is then a certification that a student performed certain activities successfully at a given college. This type of degree says something specific, providing an understanding of the recipient's minimal capabilities.

To construct curriculum in any other manner does not provide this cohesion. For instance, to adopt an array of successful curricular mechanisms is analogous to building an assembly line from individually efficient processes that have no relationship to each other. When such processes are joined, there is no possibility of a useful end product. This is what in essence happens to students today when they enter the collegiate assembly line.

Establishment of an institutional philosophy is a self-fulfilling prophecy. The principle of self-selection works in such a way that people with similar educational philosophies apply for admission and attempt to obtain administrative and teaching positions at a sympathetic college. This means that, regardless of the current position of the college, a college with an institutional philosophy will continually move toward that philosophy if it is an honest and realistic statement of goals.

Brown is an example of a school where the institutional philosophy compares poorly with the collegiate environment. The faculty is staffed largely by Ph.D.s, with a predominant emphasis upon research and publication. Brown is highly graduate and professional school oriented, having many of the better graduate departments in the country. Most of the members of the faculty sample said that the excellence of the departments or the opportunity to build an excellent department was a major reason for coming to Brown. In 1969, after more than two years of great student pressure, the Brown faculty adopted a curriculum revision. The changes in curriculum were nearly total, affecting the freshman year, abolition of requirements, examinations, grading, teaching, advising, major, senior year, and so forth. The new curriculum was progressive in outlook, giving students a great deal of freedom but also requiring a large faculty commitment to the undergraduate college and interdisciplinary work. For instance, special courses were designed for the freshman and senior year which faculty were needed to staff; grading relied upon written evaluations, which take much more time than letter grades; and the additional freedom offered students was tied to a comprehensive advising system that would require a great deal of student-faculty contact time. Faculty were, as previously indicated, unable to engage successfully in interdisciplinary teaching and unwilling to take time from their departmental activities for the new collegiate responsibilities, and no incentives were offered for such endeavors; however, the curriculum change received a great deal of publicity, and the administration played it up strongly in its admissions material. As a result, according to the admissions office, a new image was cast for Brown. In the past, Brown had been viewed by applicants as a safe or tepid "Ivy League" school. The 1970–1971 entering class, however, saw Brown as a progressive school. Applications soared past the numbers received by Yale, Harvard, and Columbia in that year, and more applicants were applying to clusters of schools like Brown, Reed, Hampshire, and Antioch. Similarly, several department chairmen said they were getting a few applications from faculty members interested as much in collegiate activities as in department activities.

Intensive interviews were conducted of a sample of approximately 10 percent of the Brown freshman class in March 1971. Three fifths of the sample said that they had come to Brown principally because of the new curriculum; most of the rest indicated the curriculum was a factor in their decision to attend. When asked how they felt about their experience at Brown, less than one quarter were positive; almost half were negative and usually bitter. The fact that over three fourths of the respondents had other than a positive reaction to the Brown curriculum, which most self-selected, is a clear indication of the poor matching of philosophy with institutional reality. A similar problem exists for the new faculty coming to Brown. Many junior people indicated that their department was negative regarding faculty participation in the freshman or upper-division interdisciplinary course except when taught as an additional course. For those who do teach on this basis, participation means less research time, and less research means denial of tenure, non-promotion, or not being rehired.

If substantive changes are not made in the real curriculum, the word eventually will spread that Brown does not offer what it promises. At this point, "progressively oriented" faculty and students will not continue to apply. In addition, confrontation may occur at the school, people who mistakenly elected to come to Brown will leave, or apathy will grow. For instance, two faculty members interviewed said they were leaving for what they believed were "really progressive" schools.

Faculty and student rationales for participating in universities were most clearly defined at universities with the most clearly defined institutional philosophies. Of the twenty-six sample schools St. John's has the most clearly defined institutional philosophy, based upon a perennialist philosophy implemented through a great books program; and the student and faculty who attended the college did so for reasons most closely associated with the institutional philosophy. As a result of the close correspondence between the institution's program and its guiding philosophy, four fifths of the students interviewed said that they were very satisfied or fairly satisfied with their St. John's experience, and all of the faculty also had a positive experience.

Lower attrition rates, and therefore lower costs, can be expected to accompany more knowledgeable selection of schools by students and faculty. St. John's is a bad example in this respect, because its catalog fails to note the isolation of its curriculum and location. This is a high cause of turnover, and the omission of such an institutional reality from the catalog should be expected to cause a large attrition. In addition, so few colleges operate with well-articulated philosophies that St. John's attracts some students simply because of its program's coherence rather than its content. Were more schools to develop explicit goals and objectives, students wishing a coherent program would have more choice. However, the success of St. John's is borne out by the fact that it is a very satisfied community, notably free of the faculty and student unrest which was so prevalent elsewhere. Therefore, one can certainly conclude, based upon the observations of twenty-six colleges, that the establishment of institutional philosophies with implementable and realistic objectives is highly necessary and desirable in providing a higher-quality undergraduate education which has greater meaning to the internal and external community while at the same time reducing college costs by cutting attrition rates.

Publicity

After a philosophy and curriculum are planned publicity both inside and outside the college is critical. It is essential that students, faculty, and administrators understand the workings and reasons for any curricular structure; however, people at almost all sample colleges were unaware of many of the features of their school's curriculum. Administrators were occasionally incredulous when told that their catalog described a program such as student-created majors; and students and faculty frequently indicated even more glaring ignorance. In MIT's two-year Unified Science Study Program, for instance, most students were unaware that their work would not fulfill general MIT requirements. The faculty and administrators' lack of familiarity with all aspects of the curriculum placed severe handicaps on their ability to provide students with

reliable advice. This problem was compounded by student ignorance. Many students, for example, described feelings of great
destructive anxiety about failing examinations which in recent years
everyone had passed. Had students been made cognizant of the low
or nonexistent failure rate, much of their anxiety would have been
dissipated, and the examinations could have been converted to an
opportunity for self-appraisal and advice; at the same time, those
faculty members who consider the examination a good way of weed-
ing out poorer students should know that this is not the case.

The power of publicity is more subtle than the effects of
budget. Each year an administrator allocates space in the catalog
and brochures and writes descriptions of the various new academic
programs or mechanisms requiring revision. Often these administrators, who are not part of the process which governs the curriculum,
have little understanding of the purpose or functioning of a new
program, and consequently relegate a poor description to isolated
and/or inappropriate spaces in the publications. What should occur
is that changes, additions, or other unique features be given priority,
since students and faculty will not think to search through the
catalog for the offerings of a new interdisciplinary program as they
would if the biology department's courses were equally hidden.
People will not expect the grading system to be other than standard
unless it is explained well and prominently. In many instances,
separate publications describing new offerings should be universally
distributed with the catalog.

In any case, program descriptions should be comprehensive.
Faculty debate before a program's approval, for example, usually
notes many potential benefits and dangers which students, administrators, and the majority of faculty who pay little attention to
most meetings should be aware of. If a senior-seminar program is
approved to lure students away from their majors, the students and
faculty should know. If there is a danger that graduate school
applicants will be hurt by a grading change, or if such fears can be
laid to rest, students should know. The lack of communication felt
by some at every school could be alleviated if university officials took
less for granted. Many students at both Sarah Lawrence and New
College expressed fear that graduation without a major would hurt
their chances with graduate schools. Administrators freely told inter-

viewers that the school's informal contacts, as well as the experience of previous students, had convinced them that their graduates would in no way be penalized. Why couldn't they tell that to their students?

Two examples help dramatize the impact of good internal publicity. Student-created majors blossomed at Brown, twenty years after the option was first made available, only because they received better publicity. A more compelling instance was found with freshman seminars. Faculty and administrators at many schools sponsoring freshman seminars expressed the hope that the small and often informal class arrangements would spawn advising relationships between the freshmen and their instructors. This hope was realized only at schools where participating faculty and students had been told explicitly that advising relationships were expected. In the other seminar programs with similar class sizes, formats, and subject matter, such relationships simply did not develop. (The only exception was that professors teaching less than five freshmen in a seminar often acted as their advisor.)

The comprehensive and enthusiastic promotion of an academic program can lead participants to believe they are beginning something special and should work especially hard to ensure its success. This was demonstrated at Harvard, where student and faculty participants had heard only rave reviews of the freshman-seminar program and therefore had a desire to make their seminar succeed, since failure could be blamed only on them. This approach can be carried too far, and the expectation can too greatly exceed the reality. Thus, Trinity and Brown attempted to use the Harvard model to publicize their seminar programs without Harvard's solid foundation of seven years of excited faculty teaching excellent courses. The resulting student disappointment at the two schools, channeled into expressions like "My seminar was awful but it's an exception" was the largest found at colleges with seminar programs. The overselling of these programs could easily boomerang, causing a bitter, mistrustful attitude toward the curriculum and its promotors.

Each college's curriculum, then, should be conspicuously, comprehensively, and honestly advertised to its population. The administrators who have contact with students, faculty, curriculum, and/or the writing of the catalog should be involved in all academic planning functions. While this is suggested here as a method of producing better-informed administrators, it can work reciprocally by providing an academic role to what have been considered non-academic positions, such as that of registrar. The registrar is, at most schools, treated as a petty record keeper, but the registrar has traditionally been the only member of the university community with complete knowledge of the faculty rules and legislation. For instance, the registrar at one of the sample schools single-handedly defeated the university's new grading system by interpreting the faculty legislation as he desired. The registrar at Brandeis was an academic who served on all academic committees with great success. Therefore, it would be valuable to have an academic, as opposed to a bookkeeper, as registrar and to place such an individual on all academic university bodies.

Prospective faculty should also be cognizant of a school's curriculum before accepting a position. Too often departmental and financial factors eclipse even the consideration of other elements. If faculty will be expected to teach in an interdisciplinary program, write detailed evaluations of their students, or be available and informed as advisors, they should certainly be informed. The major reason Eckerd's core program was more successful than the rest examined was that all prospective faculty were explicitly informed of their obligation to participate. Those who felt it too large a burden could go elsewhere.

Publicizing the curriculum outside a college is something schools can benefit from, particularly with today's labor market, which allows colleges more selectivity in hiring faculty. Colleges will be able to find the individual who is not only proficient in a specialty but also eager to work with the distinctive curricular mechanisms available.

Colleges need also to explain their academic programs to graduate schools and employers, although most sample schools with any distinctive options experienced difficulty conforming to rigid graduate admissions policies. For example, even though Reed supplements each student's transcript with a description of its unique grading system, students still have experienced some graduate school difficulty. However, students would undoubtedly have been more discriminated against if the college had neglected the explanation.

This communication is even more important for new colleges because graduate schools have had no experience with them or their graduates. Professors at Prescott, for example, founded in 1965, found that they achieved best results when they sent student references to friends teaching at graduate schools, because Prescott was unknown.

Finally, for the good of specific programs as well as the total institution, colleges should direct explanations of their curriculum to surrounding communities. This procedure not only can create better understanding but also a sharing of resources. Local agencies, businesses, and professionals, for example, can provide formal and informal independent-study opportunities as well as the resources for field work and research. In addition, local residents have skills and interests which can be brought to the campus through non-departmental course programs and less structured arrangements. Students and faculty at Tufts, Trinity, and Stanford, which involved local people in several academic programs, found the residents eager to come to the college, often without pay. Similarly, these three schools provided courses and seminars of mutual benefit to the community and their students.

The potential for good college-town communications is tremendous. Rather than regarding each other with mistrust and hostility, the college and community could begin cooperative programs. Once aware of each other's resources, they could work together on common problems, such as a housing shortage or the plentitude of dangerous drugs. For some colleges, better community relations could attract previously untapped local financial resources.

In most cases, the college and surrounding community are equally unlikely to propose a cooperative program. Yet people at Stanford and Trinity said that the small steps initiated by the college, such as providing seminars to high school students or asking a few local people to teach, were warmly welcomed by the community. At many if not most schools, these preliminary steps might be followed by further discussion, the certainty of better relations, and the possibility of a brighter future.

Bibliography

The information and conclusions in this book are derived predominantly from our visits to the twenty-six colleges. We did, however, turn to several works, both published and unpublished; and those most pertinent to this study are listed below. Studies that refer specifically to the sample colleges are listed under the name of the college.

BOWDOIN COLLEGE

Proceedings of Symposium on Undergraduate Environment, October 1962.

Senior Center Council. Reports to the faculty. 1967–1971.

WHITESIDE, W. (Charter Director of Senior Center) *The Will to Learn: Education and Community at Bowdoin.* New York: Sloan Foundation, 1970.

BRANDEIS UNIVERSITY

COHEN, J. Examination of departmental grading practices for 1964–1965, 1969–1970.

SGAN, M. "Letter Grade Achievement in Pass-Fail." *Journal of Higher Education,* 1970, *1*(8), 636–646.

151

BROWN UNIVERSITY

> MAGAZINER, I., AND MAXWELL, E. "Draft of a Working Paper for Education at Brown." 1969. Available from Student Government, Camerion Club.

CALIFORNIA INSTITUTE OF TECHNOLOGY

> "A Study of Pass/Fail Grading System at California Institute of Technology." 1970. Available from Educational Policy Committee.

CASS, J., AND BIRNBAUM, M. *Comparative Guide to American Colleges.* New York: Harper and Row, 1970.

COLUMBIA UNIVERSITY

> BELL, D. *The Reforming of General Education.* New York: Columbia University Press, 1966.

> "C.C.A. [Contemporary Civilization, first year program evaluation]—Final Report, 1967–1968." Available from Contemporary Civilization Office.

> "C.C. [Contemporary Civilization] Under Seige." *Columbia College Today,* Summer 1970.

> "Contemporary Civilization: A History and Procedure." In *Student Course Evaluation,* 1969–1970.

Committee on Educational Policy, Swarthmore College. *Critique of a College.* Swarthmore, Pa.: Swarthmore College, November 1970.

COYNE, J., AND HEBERT, T. *This Way Out.* New York: Dutton, 1972.

DAVIS, N. P. *Lawrence and Oppenheimer.* New York: Fawcett World Library, 1968.

DRESSEL, P. (Ed.) *The New Colleges.* Monograph 7. Washington, D.C. and Iowa City: American Association of Higher Education and American College Testing Program, 1971.

ECKERD COLLEGE

> Office of Institutional Research. "Distribution of Grades for Total Academic Program." 1960–1961, 1968–1969.

> Office of Institutional Research. "Faculty Grading Report." 1968.

Executive Planning Commission, University of Oklahoma. *The Future of the University.* Norman: University of Oklahoma Press, 1969.

GAFF, J., AND ASSOCIATES. *The Cluster College.* San Francisco: Jossey-Bass, 1970.

LADD, D. R. *Change in Educational Policy: Self Studies in Selected Colleges and Universities.* New York: McGraw-Hill, 1970.

MARTIN, W. B. *Conformity: Standards and Change in Higher Education.* San Francisco: Jossey-Bass, 1969.

MASSACHUSETTS INSTITUTE OF TECHNOLOGY

    MORGAN, S. "Back to the Classroom." Unpublished study of MIT sophomores who spent all or part of their freshman year in Unified Science Study Program. 1970.

    SCHWARTZ, J. (Director of Unified Science Study Program) "USSP, The First Year." 1970.

NEW COLLEGE

    Institutional self-study, 1971.

    Institutional study reports, 1964–1968.

NEWCOMB, T., AND ASSOCIATES. "The Residential College." In P. Dressel (Ed.), *New Colleges.* Monograph 7. Washington, D.C. and Iowa City: American Association of Higher Education and American College Testing Program, 1971.

PATTERSON, F., AND LONGWORTH, C. *The Making of a College* [Hampshire College, Amherst, Mass.]. Cambridge, Mass.: MIT Press, 1966.

RIESMAN, D., GUSFIELD, J., AND GAMSON, Z. *Academic Values and Mass Education.* New York: Doubleday, 1970.

ROETHLISBERGER, F. J., AND DICKSON, W. J. *Management and the Worker.* Cambridge, Mass.: Harvard University Press, 1947.

SCHOEMER, J., THOMAS, J. R., AND BRAGONIER, W. H. "Study of the Effects of Nontraditional Grades on Admission to Graduate Schools and the Awarding of Financial Assistance." *College and University,* 1973, *48*(3), 147–154.

SCHWAB, J. J. *College Curriculum and Student Protest.* Chicago: University of Chicago Press, 1969.

Select Committee on Education (C. Muscatine, Chairman). *Education at Berkeley.* Berkeley: University of California Press, 1968.

STANFORD UNIVERSITY

    Freshman Seminar Program (descriptive bulletin).

    Freshman Seminar Staff. "History of the Freshman Seminar Program." 1970. Available from the Freshman Seminar Office.

    The Stanford Daily.

    Stanford Workshops on Political and Social Issues (brochures).

    Student Center for Research in Education and Innovation. Evaluation. 1971.

SUSSMAN, W. *The Reconstruction of an American College.* New Brunswick, N.J.: Rutgers University, Office of Dean, 1968.

TAYLOR, H. *Students Without Teachers: The Crisis in the University.* New York: McGraw-Hill, 1969.

TRINITY COLLEGE

    LEE, R. "Freshman Seminar Program, 1968–1969, 1969–1970." Office of Academic Services. "Report on the Open Semester, 1970."

    PAINTER, B. "Freshman Seminar Program, 1970–1971."

    YATZKIN, A. Survey of student attitudes toward freshman seminars at Trinity. 1971.

TROW, M. "Transition from Mass to Universal Education." *Daedalus,* 1970, *99*(1), 1–43.

TUFTS UNIVERSITY

    Experimental College self-evaluation seminars, fall 1970.

    The Experimental College (twelve-page brochure).

    "Experimental College." *Tufts Alumni Review,* 1969, *15*(4).

    Experimental College Catalogue. Bulletin 17, Spring 1971.

    "Report to the Faculty of Arts and Sciences of the Ad Hoc Committee to Evaluate the Experimental College." Spring 1968.

    TREFETHEN, F. "The Experimental College of Tufts University." Report to the Provost of the University, August 7, 1970.

UNIVERSITY OF CALIFORNIA, BERKELEY EXPERIMENTAL COLLEGE PROGRAM

    SCHAAF, S. Report on the Experimental College Program. 1971.

    SUCZEK, R. F. *Best-Laid Plans.* San Francisco: Jossey-Bass, 1972.

    SUCZEK, R. F., AND ALFERT, E. *Personality Development in Two Different Education Atmospheres.* Washington, D.C.: U.S. Office of Education, 1971.

    TUSSMAN, J. *Experiment at Berkeley.* London: Oxford University Press, 1969.

UNIVERSITY OF CALIFORNIA, SANTA CRUZ

    Educational Policy Committee. Critique of grading system. 1970.

    WILSON, F. M. G. "Some Comments on the Analysis of Course Work Taken by Stevenson College Graduates." 1970.

UNIVERSITY OF MICHIGAN RESIDENTIAL COLLEGE

    FRANCIS, J. B. "Reactions of Residential College Faculty to the College, the Students, and the Core Curriculum, 1969–1970." 1970.

    MOORE, B. "Student Comments on the Core Curriculum at the Residential College, 1969–1970." 1970.

WESLEYAN UNIVERSITY

MC MAHON, J. H., HAAGEN, C. H., AND ADAMANY, D. "On Academic Standards and Procedures at Wesleyan." 1971.

YALE UNIVERSITY

BAKER, T. S. Study of graduate school opinion concerning a proposed grading change. 1971.

Committee on Honors and Special Projects. Report on special majors. 1969–1970.

Office of Educational Research. Grading information. 1965–1970.

Yale College Program of Study, 1970–1971 (catalog).

Yale College Residential Seminars, 1969–1970, 1970–1971.

Yale Course Critique.

Yale Daily News (student newspaper).

Index

A

Academic freedom, 20–21, 133, 135

ADAMANY, D., 5

Administration character, 139–141

Advising, 11–19, 68, 103, 107, 126, 129; compulsory, 14; faculty incentives for, 12–13, 16, 18; and freshman inquiry, 17–18; and general education, 11, 13–14; grading and, 14; lack of definition for, 13, 16; and major, 12, 13–14; two-part, 11–14; use of freshman seminar instructors in, 12, 15–17; use of students in, 14–15

ALFERT, E., 42

American Association of Collegiate Registrars and Admissions Officers, 110

Antioch College, 2, 136, 144; advising, 11; smorgasbord distribution, 27; student-created majors, 67, 68, 69, 70, 71; student teaching, 97–98; written evaluation, 113, 115, 116

B

Bard College, 2, 136; advising, 11, 12; divisions, 76–77, 94; general education, 27; moderation, 53–54; senior year, 57, 58; trial major, 65; written evaluation, 113

BIRNBAUM, M., 122

Bowdoin College, 2; four-point pass/fail, 119; senior center, 58–61, 62, 130; student-created major, 67, 70

BRAGONIER, W. H., 124

Brandeis University, 2, 67, 148; flexible curriculum, 83–84, 94; general education, 120; letter grades, 111, 112; partial pass/fail, 120–121

Brown University, 2, 7, 140, 143–144; advising, 11, 12, 14–15; general education, 29, 31, 32, 33, 34, 35, 36, 137, 147; group independent study projects, 100, 101, 108–109; interdepartmental majors, 67; Mei-